DRIVER'S PROTECTION MANUAL
KEEP YOUR DRIVING LICENCE

DRIVER'S PROTECTION MANUAL
KEEP YOUR DRIVING LICENCE

HARRY JONES

First published in Great Britain by Swordworks Books

ISBN 978-1-906512-42-2

Printed and bound in the UK & US

A catalogue record of this book is available from the British Library

Cover design by Swordworks Books

The roads of Great Britain present a virtual minefield for the car and motorcycle driver. Even a minor infringement of the rules can result in a fine and the inconvenience of penalty points on a licence and a possible subsequent driving ban. For the person who drives for a living, sales reps, engineers and others who use the roads in pursuit of their job or business, the results are much more serious. The private motorist who has been banned from driving can quite simply use public transport. The person that drives for a living and loses their license, or in some cases only has penalty points added to their license, may find themselves losing their livelihood completely. It is to help the drivers avoid this unhappy situation that we have assembled this book.

The plain fact is that the UK government earns substantial tax revenues by levying punitive fines on drivers. There seems to be no real concern as to whether or not the driver may suffer the severest inconvenience, or may lose their livelihood and end up as a burden on the taxpayer, by way of the unemployment queue. The parent who needs a driving license to transport their children to and from a school. Education, education, education? Not where the golden fleece of the speed camera is concerned. This is not to say that some drivers do not deserve fines and penalty points, even driving bans. Clearly some do. But equally clearly, they are entitled to the full PROTECTION of the law, as well as be subject to the full PUNISHMENT of the law.

In many cases, the speeding ticket or other offence is not reasonable. And even when it is, you are entitled to expect the police to make their case in a thoroughly legal and proper way. Often, they do not. If they fail to make a proper case, it is your right to exploit their failure to overturn the case against you.

The sole purpose of the massive and insidious system of levying fines and in other ways punishing drivers seems to be money. Government tells us that it is our safety they have in mind, but studies repeatedly show that speed cameras, and often speed limits, make absolutely no difference at all. Sometimes they slow traffic and actually cause problems. So why are they there, if not for raising money for the government.

Are there ways to avoid suffering the worst of the continual hounding of the motorist, the constant attempts to criminalise law abiding citizens? Yes, there certainly are, and number of secrets that the government and in some cases the police would prefer that drivers do not know. The furore over wealthy private motorists paying large sums of money to an expert lawyer to beat motoring court cases has been widely publicised in the media. Both the government and the police have at various times complained about the apparent ease with which some people seem to defeat the law. But are they beating the law? Surely, it is the police and government that are failing to make a case. Or do they expect us motorists to put our head in the noose without a struggle? Defeating the law is hardly uppermost in the mind of the person threatened with the loss of their licence, and possibly their business and livelihood that they have spent a great deal of time, effort and money building up.

What we offer you is the chance to open the door on a wide range of techniques and tactics that will in many cases avoid the loss of your licence, avoid a large fine and keep on the road without suffering the worst of what many people would say excessive and unjust motoring rules, rules that it may seem to the average driver are aimed at preventing them from going about their normal, daily business.

Harry Jones

CONTENTS

INTRODUCTION

This book is divided into several sections of to cover the wide range of laws and situations that the average driver is likely to find themselves falling foul of in the course of their career. We will look at the range of motoring offences, the rules and regulations of the road that often seem to be stacked higher than a City of London office block. We look at the speeding regulations, probably one of the commonest areas for the driver to get into trouble with, together with a raft of other rules and regulations, traps to collar the unwary motorist into parting with their cash, often for no reason.

Should you be unlucky enough to be prosecuted for a motoring offence, you may well find yourself in court. In this case, there are procedures that you can use to at the very least mitigate the offence for which you are being charged and received the lightest possible penalty, and in some cases avoid a conviction altogether.

We will also be taking a look at the regulations that govern the use of wheel clamps, together with parking regulations generally and how the driver can avoid having to pay excessive charges, sometimes penalty charges, merely for stopping their vehicle for some otherwise legitimate purpose. Wheel clamps seem to be the modern equivalent of the medieval 'tolls', imposed by unscrupulous landowners to force people to pay for crossing their land, even when it was the only available route from one town to another. Private tolls were eventually abolished, due to their unsavoury, seamy and underhand operation as a means of extracting money from poorer people. Now we have the wheelclamp.

Although it may not seem like it to the average driver, with what some-

9

times appears to be a campaign to harrass and punish them merely for being on the road, you do have rights. We will examine these rights so that you are able to fully understand what you can and cannot do when driving and using your vehicle.

Further chapters look into such things as speed cameras, which are sometimes highly visible and at other times virtually invisible, but always ready to trap the unwary driver with points, fines and subsequent driving bans. We will look at accidents, what to do if you are involved in one and how to avoid being blamed.

The purpose of this book is not to cheat the law. Quite to the contrary, the purpose is more to prevent the law from cheating you. You want your driving career to continue, your business to thrive and grow. What we offer will, we hope, help you to get their without being unfairly stopped along the way.

The fact is that for drivers in Great Britain there are millions of fixed penalty notices issued every year. Approximately 30% of drivers are at risk each year of being issued with a fixed penalty notice, and if you are a company driver you will stand a greater risk of this kind of penalty due to the greater mileage that you travel each year. Apart from fixed penalty notices, there are tens of thousands of motoring offences that go to court by way of the issuing of a summons. Do these punitive fines and charges make the roads any safer? Many professionals and professional organisations suggest that a large part of the revenue raised by the government in motoring fines makes no contribution whatsoever towards road safety. It's only contribution is to the taxes that the government raises.

There are a number of ways that you can avoid becoming a victim to these punitive charges. Not in every case, and not for every driver, but the object is to change the odds that are currently stacked against you and put the odds in your favour. Should you be unfortunate enough to be issued with a notice of illegal parking or speeding, you have an excellent chance of getting the note is overturned. The first thing, however, is that you are a way of how to do this in order to have the best possible chance of a successful outcome for yourself. For example, in the United

Kingdom we have the National parking adjudication service, where motorists can appeal against fixed penalty charges. It is a fact that almost two thirds of appeals have a successful outcome and resulted in the note is being dismissed.

Of course, the best way to avoid a motoring summons or fixed penalty notice is to always keep within the speed limit and to never ever park anywhere other than in authorised parking bays. In practical terms, this is of course quite impossible with the state of Britain's congested roads and decreasing number of parking spaces. There are times when drivers have no choice other than to stretch the law to its very limits in order to just get from A to B. In those cases, we aim to offer some advice and solutions that will help to avoid punitive action where possible.

ONE

MOTORING OFFENCES

Once the driver is stopped by the police for an offence they will immediately fall foul of the system that is incredibly complicated and difficult to understand. Later in this chapter we give lists and examples of all the different types of offences that you could be accused of and it is a very long list indeed. If you are stopped by the police the first thing to remember is that losing your temper of becoming angry is not calculated to win you any friends of gain any advantage. In order to get off to the best possible start and make the best of a bad situation, it is vital that you are polite and treat the police officer with courtesy and consideration. Insults and abuse will only get their backup and make them more likely to ensure that you are reported for the maximum number of offences they are able to think up.

There are some rules you need to consider that go beyond normal courtesy. The traffic policeman will have seen hundreds, thousands, possibly tens of thousands of motorists, many with similar offences as the one that they are stopping you for. Lying to this officer is totally pointless and stupid. If you can't think of anything to say, say nothing. And certainly do not ever, ever admit the offence. If the officer has not told you why he has stopped you, ask them for the reason to be explained to you. If you feel that the offence you are being accused of is one that you have not committed, say so and be adamant , but do this politely. The important thing to remember is to be brief, polite and to the point.

It would be reasonable, for example, to say that you are certain that you were travelling at a lower speed than the speed limit. If the traffic officer makes a note of that it can only serve you well in a future defence. But do not estimate your speed, when the officer has this on paper it is something that they can use to argue with you later. There is always the possibility that if you say that you are certain you are under the speed limit the traffic officer may, in your particular case, be unable to provide supporting evidence that you were committing an offence. This does happen on occasion. The important fact here is never ever admit your guilt. In many situations the traffic officer will issue you with a fixed penalty ticket, or in some cases say that they will be reporting you for consideration of a summons. If this is the case you have no choice but to accept it politely but do insist on knowing exactly what is the offence that he is alleging. You need to bear in mind that whatever you say at this stage may be valuable in any future defence, or should you say the wrong thing, could harm any future defence. If you have nothing useful to say, say nothing.

You may or may not realise that traffic police do have discretion when making a decision about reporting a traffic offence or issuing a fixed penalty ticket. In this respect you should realise that your conduct at the roadside when stopped by the police is absolutely vital, both in the possibility of avoiding prosecution completely there and then or by establishing a sound basis for future defence of your ticket or summons.

It is essential that you stay calm, polite and considerate, we cannot stress this enough, it could be the difference between innocence and guilt, prosecution or going free.

On the question of the police officer that does speak to you about an alleged motoring offence, it is always a good idea to get details of that officer and the date, time and place of where you have been stopped. To identify the police officer, his collar number will be sufficient. In addition, it may be as well for you to write down details of road conditions, is the road quiet or busy, wet or dry, is visibility poor or good? The more information you have, the better it will serve later.

If you are issued with a fixed penalty ticket these, as the name suggests, will have a fixed financial penalty which you will be liable to pay. More serious fixed penalty tickets will be coloured yellow and this means that they carry an endorsement on your licence. Less serious fixed penalty tickets are white. If you are issued with one of these tickets, and of course make certain that you have not admitted the offence, you then need to make a decision as to whether admit it or defend. If you do admit the offence you have a fixed period of time, normally within 28 days, to fill in the slip at the bottom of the ticket and send it with the amount of the fine to the address given. It is essential that you do not stray outside of this time period as this could result in more serious action being taken against you including a warrant for her arrest.

If you decide to defend the ticket then you need to indicate this also within the given time period. You should bear in mind that if you do decide to defend the ticket there will be additional cost to yourself. These could include the costs of a solicitor to defend yourself and possible prosecution costs if you are still found guilty. There is also the possibility of the initial penalty being increased at the subsequent court appearance. Therefore this is a decision that does not to be taken lightly and you must weigh up the possibilities of being found not guilty against the possible increased costs if you are found guilty. In many cases it is of course likely to depend on the severity of the offence for which you have been reported. If it is a minor parking offence with no possible endorsement you may be well advised to simply pay the penalty and just live to fight another day. If it is a more serious endorsable offence and you already have points on your licence, possibly that many points that convictions of this offence could result in a driving ban, then clearly this will influence your decision and you may well consider that a strong defence against the ticket is worthwhile.

Table of ACPO guidelines for issuing FPN's for speeding offences at given speeds.

Speed Limit (mph)	Fixed Penalty Notice (mph)	Court Summons (mph)
20	25	35
30	35	50
40	46	66
50	57	76
60	68	86
70	79	96

You should note that Fixed Penalty Notices (endorsable or otherwise) DO NOT EQUAL A CRIMINAL RECORD. The only exception to this is very serious offences, driving while disqualified, causing death by dangerous driving etc.

The first step in trying to get a fixed penalty ticket revoked is to write to the police superintendent in the area in which you were reported for committing the offence. The superintendent will confer with the officer that issued the ticket and then make a decision as to whether to revoke it or not. Quite a large number of fixed penalty tickets are revoked every year, and so this is a possibility that is always worth exploring.

If you are issued with a fixed penalty ticket for an endorsable offence, the police officer that stops you will ask you to produce your driving licence. They will then use this to assess whether the offence carries sufficient points that when combined with existing points you have on your licence could mean that you are likely to be disqualified under the totting up procedure. In that case you would be issued with a summons, as offences that may result in a driving ban cannot be dealt with under the fixed penalty scheme. In addition, if your licence is likely to be endorsed the police will want possession of it to send off for the endorsement to be added. It is unwise to part with your driving licence at the time when you are stopped as this could suggest to a later court hearing that you felt that you were guilty. It is not an admission of guilt as such but you do not of course want to give the impression of guilt to a future magistrates hearing. All you need to do is to offer to produce your driving licence at a police station within the time given. This is allowed by law, there is no absolute requirement to carry a driving licence, only to produce it within a given time period.

When you do go to the police station, only surrender your licence if you have decided that you are not going to defend the case. If you have decided to defend it, produce the licence but do not surrender it. If you do surrender it is likely that it will still be sent away for endorsement. In cases where you do not admit to the offence, the issue will then come to court to be decided there.

Driving Licence Penalty Points and Disqualification
Driving licence holders may be penalised following conviction by a court for offences committed on the road with a motor vehicle.

Penalties range from:

- the issue of fixed penalty notices for non-endorsable offences (which do not require a court appearance unless the charge is contested and incur no driving license penalty points although the relevant fixed penalty has to be paid)

- to those for endorsable offences when penalty points are added on the license counterpart and the fixed penalty is incurred or a heavy fine imposed on conviction if a court appearance is made

17

In other cases, licence disqualification, and in serious instances imprisonment, may follow conviction in a magistrates' court or indictment in a higher court. Holders of vocational driving entitlements may be separately penalised for relevant offences, which could result in such entitlements being suspended or revoked. In serious circumstances the holder may be disqualified from holding a vocational entitlement.

The Penalty Points System on Conviction and Disqualification

The Road Traffic Offenders Act 1988 (with further provisions relating to driving offences in the Road Traffic Act 1991) prescribes penalty points following conviction for motoring offences. The penalty points system grades road traffic offences according to their seriousness on a scale from 2 to 10 points. Once a maximum of 12 penalty points has accumulated within a three year period from the date of the first offence to the current offence, disqualification of the licence for at least six months is automatic.

Most offences rate a fixed number of penalty points to ensure consistency and to simplify the administration, but a discretionary range applies to a few offences where the gravity may vary from one case to another. Unless the court decides otherwise, when a driver is convicted of more than one offence at the same hearing, only the points relative to the most serious offence will normally be endorsed on the licence. Once a period of disqualification has been imposed, the driver starts fresh and those points will not be counted again.

To discourage repeated offences however, the courts impose progressively longer disqualification periods in future instances of maximum accrued points.

- 12 months for subsequent disqualifications within three years
- 24 months for a third disqualification within three years

Licence Endorsement Codes and Penalty Points

Following conviction for an offence, the driver's licence green counterpart will be endorsed by the convicting court with a code and number of penalty points imposed.

Disqualification

The endorsing of penalty points will also arise on conviction for offences where disqualification is discretionary. In this case the offender's driving licence will be endorsed with four points. The courts are still free to disqualify immediately if the circumstances justify

Offences (Road Traffic Offenders Act 1988, Schedule 2) carrying obligatory disqualification include:-

- Causing death by dangerous driving and manslaughter.
- Dangerous driving within three years of a similar conviction.
- Driving or attempting to drive while unfit through drink or drugs.
- Driving or attempting to drive with more than the permitted breath- alcohol level.
- Failure to provide a breath, blood or urine specimen.
- Racing and speed trials on the highway.

Driving while disqualified is a serious offence that can result in a fine at level five on the standard scale, six months imprisonment, or both.

Special Reasons for Non-disqualification

The courts have discretion in exceptional mitigating circumstances not to impose a disqualification. The mitigating circumstance must not be one

19

which attempts to make the offence appear less serious and no account will be taken of hardship, other than exceptional hardship. Pleading that you have a wife and children to support or that you will lose your job is not generally considered to be exceptional hardship.

If account has previously been taken of circumstances in mitigation of a disqualification, the same circumstances cannot be considered again within three years.

Where a court decides in exceptional circumstances, not to disqualify a convicted driver, four penalty points will be added to the driver's licence in lieu of the disqualification.

Driving Offences
Dangerous Driving

Since 1st July 1992 "reckless driving" has been termed "dangerous" driving.

Such a charge may be levied if: –

> *"the driving falls far short of what would be expected of a competent and careful driver, and it would be obvious to a competent and careful driver that driving in that way would be dangerous"*

or

> *"If it was obvious to a competent and careful driver, that driving the vehicle in its current state would be dangerous."*

"Dangerous" refers to danger either of injury to any person or of serious damage to property. The principal offences to which this relates are dangerous driving and causing death by dangerous driving.

Interfering with Vehicles

It is an offence for any person to cause danger to road users by way of intentionally and without lawful authority placing objects on a road, interfering with motor vehicles, or directly or indirectly interfering with traffic equipment such as road signs.

Penalties

Penalties are heavy. Causing death by careless driving while under the influence of drink or drugs carries a maximum penalty of up to five years in prison and/or a fine.

For causing a danger to road users the maximum penalty is up to seven years' imprisonment and/or a fine.

In addition to disqualification and the endorsement of penalty points, courts may impose fines and, for certain offences, imprisonment. The maximum fine for most offences is determined by reference to a scale set out in the Criminal Justice Act 1991. Offences such as dangerous driving, failing to stop after an accident or failure to report an accident, and drink-driving offences, carry the maximum fine, as do certain vehicle construction, use offences (overloading, insecure loads, using a vehicle in a dangerous condition) and using a vehicle without insurance.

New Driver Penalties

The Road Traffic (New Drivers) Act 1995 concerns drivers who passed their driving test on or after 1st June 1997. Where such drivers acquire six or more penalty points within two years of passing the test the DVLA will automatically revoke the licence on notification by a court or fixed penalty office. Such drivers have to surrender their full licence and obtain a provisional licence to start driving again as a learner. They will have to pass both the theory and practical tests again.

Penalty points counting towards the total of six include any incurred before passing the test, if this was not more than three years before the latest penalty point offence. Points imposed after the probationary period will also count if the offence was committed during that period. Passing the retest will not remove the penalty points from the licence.

Short Period Disqualification (SPD)

If a driver is disqualified for less than 56 days, the court will stamp the counterpart of his driving licence and return it to him. The stamp will show how long disqualification is to last. The licence does not have to be renewed when the SPD ends - it becomes valid again the day following expiration of the disqualification.

Removal of Penalty Points and Disqualifications

Penalty points can be removed after a specified waiting period - four years from the date of the offence, except in the case of reckless/ dangerous driving convictions when the four years is taken from the date of conviction. Endorsements for alcohol-related offences must remain on a licence for 11 years. Licences returned after disqualification will show no penalty points but previous disqualifications (within four years) will remain and if a previous alcohol/drugs driving offence disqualification has been incurred, this will remain on the license for 11 years. Application may be made for reinstatement after varying periods depending on the duration of the disqualification as follows:-

- less than two years - no prior application time
- less than four years - after two years have elapsed
- between four years and ten years - after half the time has elapsed
- in other cases - after five years have elapsed

The courts are empowered to require a disqualified driver to retake the driving test. Following the introduction of provisions contained in the Road Traffic Act 1991 it is now mandatory for the courts to impose "extended" re-tests for the most serious offences, namely dangerous driving, causing death by dangerous driving and manslaughter by the driver of a motor vehicle (in Scotland, the charge is culpable homicide).

Re-tests for Offending Drivers

Where drivers are convicted of the offences of manslaughter, causing death by dangerous driving or dangerous driving and mandatory disqualification is imposed, an "extended" re-test (involving at least one hour's driving) must be taken. This also applies to drivers disqualified by penalty points. Courts may order drivers disqualified for lesser offences to take an ordinary driving test.

Drink-Driving and Breath Tests

It is an offence to drive or to attempt to drive when the level of alcohol in the breath is more than 35 micrograms per 100 millilitres. This is determined by means of an initial breath test, conducted on the spot when the driver is stopped, and later substantiated by a breath-testing machine (Lion Intoximeter) at a police station. The breath/alcohol limit equates to the blood/alcohol limit of 80 milligrams of alcohol in 100 millilitres of blood or the urine/alcohol limit of 107 milligrams of alcohol in 100 millilitres of urine.

Failure to Produce a Breath Sample and Low Breath-Rest Readings

If the person suspected of an alcohol-related offence cannot due to health reasons produce a breath sample, or if a breath test shows a reading of not more than 50 micrograms of alcohol per 100 millilitres of breath, he is given the opportunity of an alternative test, either blood or urine, for laboratory analysis. This test can only be carried out at a police station or a hospital and the decision as to which alternative is chosen rests with the police (unless a doctor present determines a blood test cannot or should not be taken). Similarly, if a breath test of a driver shows the proportion of alcohol to be no more than 50 micrograms in 100 millilitres of breath, the driver can request an alternative test (blood or urine).

23

Prosecution for Drink-Driving Offences

Prosecution will follow test failure, resulting in a fine or imprisonment and automatic disqualification from driving. Failure to submit to a breath test and to a blood or urine test are serious offences, and drivers will find themselves liable to heavy penalties on conviction and potentially long-term disqualification or driving licence endorsement (endorsements for such offences remain on a driving license for eleven years).

The police do not have powers to carry out breath tests at random but they do have powers to enter premises to require a breath test from a person suspected of driving while impaired, or who has been driving or been in charge of a vehicle that has been involved in an accident in which another person has been injured.

Drink-Driving Disqualification

Conviction for a first drink-driving offence will result in a minimum one year period of disqualification; a second or subsequent offence longer periods of disqualification. If the previous conviction took place within ten years of the current offence the disqualification must be for at least three years.

Drivers convicted twice for drink-driving offences may have their driving licences revoked altogether. Offenders who are disqualified twice within a ten-year period and those found to have an exceptionally high level of alcohol in the body (more than two and a half times over the limit), or those who twice refuse to provide a specimen, will be classified as high-risk offenders (HROs) by the Driver and Vehicle Licensing Agency. They will be required to show that they no longer have an "alcohol problem" by means of a medical examination (including blood analysis of liver enzymes) by a DVLA-approved doctor before licence restoration.

Penalties Against Vocational Entitlements

Where a licence holder is disqualified from driving following conviction for offences committed with cars or other light vehicles, or as a result of penalty points, any vocational entitlement held is automatically lost until the licence is reinstated. Additionally, the holder of an LGV/PCV vocational entitlement may have this revoked or suspended by the DVLA without reference to the Traffic Commissioner (TC) and be disqualified from holding such entitlement, for a fixed or indefinite period, at any time, on the grounds of misconduct or physical disability. Furthermore, a person can be refused a new LGV/PCV driving entitlement following licence revocation, again either indefinitely or for some other period of time which the Secretary of State (via the DVLA) specifies. A new vocational test may be ordered before the entitlement is restored.

Disqualification from holding an LGV vocational entitlement does not prevent a licence holder from continuing to drive vehicles within the category B and C1 entitlements.

The TCs continue to play a disciplinary role in regard to driver conduct, but only at the request of the DVLA. They have powers to call drivers to a public inquiry (PI) to give information and to answer questions as to their conduct. Their duty is to report back to the DVLA if they consider that an LGV/PCV entitlement should be revoked or the holder disqualified from holding an entitlement - the DVLA must follow the TC's recommendation in these matters.

Failure to attend a PI when requested to do so (unless a reasonable excuse is given) means that the DVLA will automatically refuse a new vocational entitlement or suspend or revoke an existing one.

Large Goods Vehicle (LGV) drivers who have been off the road for a period of time, after being disqualified, must prove themselves capable of driving small goods vehicles legally and safely for a period of time before their LGV driving entitlement may be restored by the TCs.

Rules on disciplining LGV entitlement holders require TCs to follow a set of recommended guidelines in imposing penalties. Under these rules, and where there are no aggravating circumstances, a driver being disqualified for twelve months or less should be sent a warning letter with no further disqualification of the LGV entitlement. Where a driving disqualification is for more than one year, the offender should be called to appear before the TC and he should incur an additional suspension, amounting to between one and three months. The intention is to allow the person to regain his driving skills and road sense in a car before driving a heavy vehicle again. Where two or more driving disqualifications of more than eight weeks have been incurred within the past five years, and the combined total of disqualification exceeds twelve months, the driver should be called to a PI and a further period of LGV driving disqualification imposed amounting to between three and six months. In the case of new LGV entitlements, for applicants with nine or more penalty points on their ordinary licence, the guidelines recommend the TC issue a warning as to future conduct or suggest that the applicant tries again when the penalty points total has been reduced.

Removal of LGV Driving Licence Disqualification

Drivers disqualified from holding an LGV/PCV entitlement may apply to have the disqualification removed after two years if it was for less than four years, or after half the period if the disqualification was for more than four years but less than ten. In any other case, including disqualification for an indefinite period, an application for its removal cannot be made for five years. If an application for the removal fails, another application cannot be made for three months. The DVLA will not necessarily readily restore LGV/PCV driving entitlements on application following disqualification. An applicant may be called to a PI by a TC who will inquire into the events which led to the disqualification and who may also decide that the applicant must wait longer before applying again, must spend a period driving small (up to 7.5 ton) vehicles, or must take a new LGV/PCV driving test to regain the vocational entitlement.

Appeals

If the DVLA refuses to grant an application for an LGV/PCV driving entitlement or revokes, suspends or limits an existing entitlement, the applicant or entitlement holder may appeal under the Road Traffic Act 1988. He must notify the DVLA and any TC involved of his intention to appeal. The appeal can then be made to a magistrates' court acting for the petty sessions in England or Wales, or in Scotland to the local sheriff.

Road Traffic Offences and Legal Action

When road traffic-related offences are committed alternative procedures may be followed by the police (or traffic wardens where appropriate) in the way of legal action. Depending on the nature of the offence, the offender may be issued with a fixed-penalty notice or reported for prosecution and required to answer directly to the court.

Fixed-penalty System

Fixed-penalty notices (tickets) may be issued for a large number of traffic, motoring and vehicle offences. Generally these will be issued by the police but traffic wardens are empowered to do so for some offences. When offences are committed, the driver is given a notice which specifies the offence, an indication whether it is a driving license endorsable or non-endorsable offence (by the notice colour and wording), and the penalty which has to be paid. If the driver is not available the ticket may be attached to the vehicle windscreen, but the driver is still responsible for payment. Should the driver of a vehicle fail to pay, responsibility for payment rests with the registered vehicle keeper (the person/company whose name is on the registration document).

Fixed-penalty Procedure

The police (and to a certain extent, the traffic wardens) operate the fixed-penalty system for dealing with road traffic and related offences. Some 250 motoring offences are included, divided into driving licence endorsable and non-endorsable offences. The former involves the police issuing a yellow penalty ticket for which a penalty is payable and the driving licence being confiscated and returned with the appropriate penalty points added when the penalty is paid.

If the offender does not have his driving licence with him a penalty notice will not be issued there but at the police station when the licence is produced within seven days. For non-endorsable offences a white ticket (involving a lesser penalty) is issued to the driver, if present, or is fixed to the vehicle. Any driver who receives a fixed-penalty notice (yellow or white) can elect to have the matter dealt with by a court to defend himself or to put forward mitigating circumstances. Alternatively he can accept guilt and pay the penalty. However, failure to pay within the requisite period (twenty eight days) will result in the penalties being increased by 50%. In this case the increased amount becomes a fine and non-payment will lead to arrest and a court appearance.

Offences include:
Yellow Ticket (endorsable)
- Speeding.
- Contravention of motorway regulations.
- Defective vehicle components (brakes, steering, tyres) and vehicle in a dangerous condition.
- Contravention of traffic signs.
- Insecure and dangerous loads.
- Leaving vehicles in dangerous positions.
- Contravention of pedestrian rights.
- White ticket (non-endorsable)
- Not wearing seat belt.
- Driving and stopping offences (reversing, parking, towing).
- Contravention of traffic signs, box junctions, bus lanes.
- Contravening driving prohibitions.
- Vehicle defects (brakes, steering, speedometer, wipers).
- Contravening exhaust and noise regulations.
- Exceeding weight limits (overloading).

- Contravention of vehicle lighting requirements.
- Contravention of vehicle excise requirements.

This is only a summary of an extensive list of offences. Failure to pay a fixed penalty within the prescribed period can result in a fine, unless a statutory statement of ownership or of fact (to the effect that he was not the legal owner of the vehicle at the time the alleged offence was committed or that, if he was the owner, the vehicle was being used without his permission) has been given to the police in whose area the original offence was committed.

Prosecution

Where one of the following road traffic offences is committed, the offender must be warned of possible prosecution at the time (unless an accident occurred at that time or immediately afterwards) or alternatively, within fourteen days, must be served with either a Notice of Intended Prosecution or a summons for the offence:-

- Dangerous, careless, inconsiderate driving.
- Failure to comply with traffic signs or the directions of a police con stable on traffic duty.
- Leaving a vehicle in a dangerous position.
- Notice of Intended Prosecution

The Notice of Intended Prosecution must be in writing and must specify the offence, the time and place committed. It must be served on the driver who committed the offence or the registered keeper of the vehicle. If, after due diligence, the police are unable to trace the vehicle driver or registered keeper within fourteen days, action can still be taken to bring about a prosecution. If, as a result of the offence (or immediately after the offence was committed) an accident occurs, there is no requirement to serve a Notice of Intended Prosecution.

The Summons

In the case of offences other than those listed, such as those committed immediately before or at the time of an accident, a summons (to answer the charges before the court) should normally be issued within six months of the date of the offence.

But in the case of certain offences:-

- obtaining a driving licence while disqualified
- driving while disqualified
- using an uninsured vehicle
- forging a driving licence or test and insurance certificates
- making false statements in connection with driving licences, test and insurance certificates

Proceedings may be brought for up to three years for these offences.

The summons will give details of the offence including when and where it took place. The court to hear the case will be named within six months. The recipient of a summons must respond as follows:-

- appear in court in person on the appointed day and make a plea of guilty or not guilty
- appoint a legal representative to appear in court and make a plea on his behalf
- plead guilty in writing to the court and allow the case to be heard in his absence (in certain cases the court may adjourn the hearing and summon the defendant to appear in person)

A not guilty plea cannot be accepted in writing. The offender must surrender his driving licence when required to do so to the court, either by delivering it in person or by sending it by post to arrive on the day prior to the hearing or by having it with him at the hearing. Failure to do so is an offence and the licence will be suspended from the time its production was required and until it is produced (thus to continue driving with it is a further offence). Where a person fails to produce his licence to the court as required, the police will request its production and will seize it and hand it over to the court.

Court Hearing

Depending on the nature of the offence, the court may hear the case in the absence of the offender and accept a written plea of guilty with a statement of mitigating circumstances. Alternatively, the hearing may be suspended pending the personal appearance of the offender. Following the hearing, a verdict will be reached. If the offender is judged not guilty the matter is ended.

If the offender is found guilty, a summary conviction is made. If the case concerns an indictable offence (one which must be tried before a jury) the accused may be bailed or remanded for the case to be heard by the Crown Court. On conviction (indictment) by the court, a penalty will be imposed (a fine or imprisonment or both) as appropriate. The driver may be disqualified from driving or have his licence endorsed with an appropriate number of penalty points.

Where an offence requires obligatory disqualification under the Road Traffic Offenders Act 1988, 34{1} but for special reasons the court decides not to impose that penalty it must, as an alternative, endorse a penalty of four points on the offender's driving licence. Further offences under the Road Traffic Act 1988 allow the courts a discretionary power of disqualification with the alternative of the obligatory endorsement of a specified number of penalty points on the offender's licence.

12-point Disqualification

The penalty points system does not alter the mandatory disqualification procedure on conviction for serious offences. Also, disqualification of the driving licence will automatically follow, for a minimum of six months, when twelve or more penalty points are accrued in a period of three years counting from the date of the first offence to the current offence and NOT from the date of conviction.

Subsequent Disqualifications

When a driver has been disqualified once, any subsequent disqualifications within three years (preceding the date of the latest offence - not conviction) will be for progressively longer periods.

The court has discretion to disqualify for a period of less than the normal six month minimum or not to disqualify when twelve points are endorsed on a licence in exceptional circumstances but in such cases it is required to endorse the driving licence with four penalty points.

Special Reasons for Non-Disqualification

The court has discretion in exceptional mitigating circumstances not to impose an obligatory disqualification. However, the mitigating circumstances must not be of a nature which appears to make the offence not serious, and no account must be taken of hardship other than exceptional hardship. Furthermore, if account has previously been taken of circumstances in mitigation of a disqualification, the same circumstance cannot be considered again within three years.

Other Reasons for Non-Disqualification

Where a person is convicted of an offence requiring obligatory disqualification and he can prove to the court that he did not know and had no reasonable cause to suspect that his actions would result in an offence being committed, the court must not disqualify him or order any penalty points to be endorsed on his driving licence.

Removal of Disqualification

Disqualifications may be removed from a driving licence after the following periods:-

- If disqualification for less than four years - after two years.
- If disqualification for four years to ten years - after half the period.
- If disqualification for more than ten years - after five years.

Penalty Points System (not applicable in Northern Ireland)

When drivers are convicted of offences where the court has discretion about imposing a disqualification but is obliged to endorse a licence, the endorsement takes the form of a number of penalty points. The number of points varies according to a scale ranging from two to ten points depending on the seriousness of the offence (as specified in Schedule 2 of the Road Traffic Offenders Act 1988). When the court convicts a driver of more than one offence at the same hearing, only the points relative to the most serious of the offences will be endorsed - the points relative to each individual offence will not be aggregated.

Removal of Penalty Points

If a driver is convicted for an offence and is disqualified from driving, any existing penalty points on the licence will be erased. The driver will then start again with a "clean slate" except that subsequent disqualifications will be for a longer period.

When the time interval between one endorsement on a licence and a subsequent endorsement is greater than three years (from the date of each offence), the earlier points no longer count towards disqualification.

Penalty-point endorsements (and disqualifications) shown on driving licences can be removed by applying for the issue of a new license after the following periods of time:-

- • Disqualifications and offences other than those below - after four years from the date of the offence (from the date of conviction in the case of a disqualification).

- • Reckless driving offences - after four years from the date of conviction.

- • Drink-driving offences - after eleven years.

Penalty Points

Section of Road Traffic Act 1998 creating offence	Description	Number of penalty points
2 3	Reckless driving (1st offence in 3 years) (now replaced by a dangerous driving offence under the RTA 1991 {s 1})	4
3	Careless or inconsiderate driving	3-9
5(2)	Being in charge of motor vehicle when unfit through drink or drugs	10
5(1)(b)	Being in charge of motor vehicle with excess alcohol in breath/blood/urine	10
6	Failing to provide specimen for breath test	4
7	Failing to provide specimen for analysis	10
22	Leaving vehicle in dangerous position	3
35/36	Failing to comply with traffic directions and signs	3

42	Contravention of construction and use regulations	3
87(1)	Driving without license	2
96	Driving with uncorrected defective eyesight or refusing eyesight test	2
97	Failing to comply with conditions of license	2
103(1)	Driving while disqualified (by order of court)	6
143	Using motor vehicle uninsured and unsecured against third-party risks	6-8
170(4)	Failing to stop after accident	8-10
178	Taking in Scotland a motor vehicle without consent or lawful authority or driving, or allowing oneself to be carried in, a motor vehicle so taken	8

Other Penalties

The courts may also impose fines and, for certain offences imprisonment, or in serious cases both. Drivers convicted twice for drink/driving-related offences may have their licences revoked altogether. Offenders found with exceptionally high levels of alcohol in their breath/blood will be classed by the DVLA as being "special risk" and will have to show that they no longer have an "alcohol problem" before their licences are restored to them.

Drinking and Driving

It is an offence to drive or to attempt to drive or to be in charge of a motor vehicle when unfit because of the effects of drink or drugs. The maximum permitted level of alcohol in the breath is 35 micrograms per 100 millilitres of breath. This equates to a blood/alcohol limit of 80 milligrams of alcohol in 100 millilitres of blood and the urine limit of 107 milligrams of alcohol in 100 millilitres of urine.

Breath Tests

A police constable in uniform may arrest any person who is in charge of, driving or attempting to drive a vehicle on a public road (or other public place) while unfit through drink or drugs. A constable may request any such person to take a breath test if he has reasonable cause to suspect the person of having alcohol in his body or of having committed a traffic offence while the vehicle was in motion or if the person was driving or attempting to drive a vehicle at the time of an accident.

If a breath test proves positive, the person will be requested to provide a further breath sample at a police station (or may be taken there under arrest if appropriate) and may be held there until fit to drive or only released if there is no likelihood of him driving while still unfit. If the second sample exceeds the limit, prosecution will follow and on the basis of evidence provided by the breath analysis a conviction may be made by the court, resulting in mandatory disqualification from driving plus a possible fine or imprisonment or both.

A person who for health reasons cannot provide a breath sample may request a blood test. So, may persons whose breath analyses show not more than 50 micrograms of alcohol per 100 millilitres of breath. It is an offence to refuse to provide a breath test or a sample of blood or urine.

Drink-Driving Disqualification

Conviction for a drink-driving offence will result in a driving licence disqualification for at least one year. Conviction for a second or subsequent offence of driving or attempting to drive under the influence of drink or drugs will result in longer periods of disqualification. If the previous conviction took place within ten years of the current offence the driver must be disqualified for at least three years.

For your information, here is a full list of Motoring Offence Codes.

Accident offences: AC10 & 20: 5-10 penalty Points. AC30: 4-9 Penalty Points.

- AC10 Failing to stop after an accident
- AC12 Aiding, Abetting, Counselling Or Procuring Ac10
- AC14 Causing Or Permitting Ac10
- AC16 Inciting Ac10
- AC20 Failing To Report An Accident Within 24 Hours
- AC22 Aiding, Abetting, Counselling Or Procuring Ac20
- AC24 Causing Or Permitting Ac20
- AC26 Inciting Ac20
- AC30 Undefined Accident Offence
- AC32 Aiding, Abetting, Counselling Or Procuring Ac30
- AC34 Causing Or Permitting Ac30
- AC36 Inciting Ac30

Disqualified driver: BA10 & 30: 6 Penalty Points.

- BA10 Driving While Disqualified
- BA12 Aiding, Abetting, Counselling Or Procuring Ba10
- BA14 Causing Or Permitting Ba10
- BA16 Inciting Ba10
- BA20 Driving While Disqualified By Reason Of Age
- BA22 Aiding, Abetting, Counselling Or Procuring Ba20

- BA24 Causing Or Permitting Ba20
- BA26 Inciting Ba20
- BA30 To Attempt To Drive While Disqualified
- BA32 Aiding, Abetting, Counselling Or Procuring Ba30
- BA34 Causing Or Permitting Ba30
- BA36 Inciting Ba30

Careless driving: CD10, 20 & 30: 3-9 Penalty Points. CD40, 50, 60 & 70: 3-11 Penalty Points.

- CD10 Driving Without Due Care And Attention
- CD12 Aiding, Abetting, Counselling Or Procuring Cd10
- CD14 Causing Or Permitting Cd10
- CD16 Inciting Cd10
- CD20 Driving Without Reasonable Consideration
- CD22 Aiding, Abetting, Counselling Or Procuring Cd20
- CD24 Causing Or Permitting Cd20
- CD26 Inciting Cd20
- CD30 Driving Without Due Care/Att. Or Consideration
- CD32 Aiding, Abetting, Counselling Or Procuring Cd30
- CD34 Causing Or Permitting Cd30
- CD36 Inciting Cd30
- CD40 Causing Death Through Careless Driving When Drunk
- CD42 Aiding, Abetting, Counselling Or Procuring Cd40
- CD44 Causing Or Permitting Cd40
- CD46 Inciting Cd40
- CD50 Causing Death By Careless Driving Through Drugs
- CD52 Aiding, Abetting, Counselling Or Procuring Cd50
- CD54 Causing Or Permitting Cd50
- CD56 Inciting Cd50
- CD60 Causing Death By Careless Driving Over Drink Limit

- CD62 Aiding, Abetting, Counselling Or Procuring Cd60
- CD64 Causing Or Permitting Cd60
- CD66 Inciting Cd60
- CD70 Causing Death By Careless Driving And No Specimen
- CD72 Aiding, Abetting, Counselling Or Procuring Cd70
- CD74 Causing Or Permitting Cd70
- CD76 Inciting Cd70

Construction and use offences: CU10, 20, 30, 40, 50 & 80: 3 Penalty Points.

- CU10 Using A Vehicle With Defective Brakes
- CU12 Aiding, Abetting, Counselling Or Procuring Cu10
- CU14 Causing Or Permitting Cu10
- CU16 Inciting Cu10
- CU20 Dangerous Cond. Of Vehicle.(Ex. Brakes/Steering/Tyres)
- CU22 Aiding, Abetting, Counselling Or Procuring Cu20
- CU24 Causing Or Permitting Cu20
- CU26 Inciting Cu20
- CU30 Using A Vehicle With Defective Tyres
- CU32 Aiding, Abetting, Counselling Or Procuring Cu30
- CU34 Causing Or Permitting Cu30
- CU36 Inciting Cu30
- CU40 Using A Vehicle With Defective Steering
- CU42 Aiding, Abetting, Counselling Or Procuring Cu40
- CU44 Causing Or Permitting Cu40
- CU46 Inciting Cu40
- CU50 Causing Danger By Reason Of Load Or Passengers
- CU52 Aiding, Abetting, Counselling Or Procuring Cu50
- CU54 Causing Or Permitting Cu50
- CU56 Inciting Cu50

- CU60 Fail To Comply With Construct. And Use Regulations
- CU62 Aiding, Abetting, Counselling Or Procuring Cu60
- CU64 Causing Or Permitting Cu60
- CU66 Inciting Cu60
- CU80 Using Mobile Phone While Driving A Motor Vehicle

Reckless/dangerous driving: DD40, 60 & 80: 3-11 Penalty Points.

- DD10 Driving In A Dangerous Manner
- DD12 Aiding, Abetting, Counselling Or Procuring Dd10
- DD14 Causing Or Permitting Dd10
- DD16 Inciting Dd10
- DD20 Driving At A Dangerous Speed
- DD22 Aiding, Abetting, Counselling Or Procuring Dd20
- DD24 Causing Or Permitting Dd20
- DD26 Inciting Dd20
- DD30 Reckless Driving
- DD32 Aiding, Abetting, Counselling Or Procuring Dd30
- DD34 Causing Or Permitting Dd30
- DD36 Inciting Dd30
- DD40 Driving In A Dangerous Manner/Speed/Recklessly
- DD42 Aiding, Abetting, Counselling Or Procuring Dd40
- DD44 Causing Or Permitting Dd40
- DD46 Inciting Dd40
- DD50 Causing Death By Dangerous Driving
- DD52 Aiding, Abetting, Counselling Or Procuring Dd50
- DD54 Causing Or Permitting Dd50
- DD56 Inciting Dd50
- DD60 Culpable Homicide While Driving A Vehicle
- DD62 Aiding, Abetting, Counselling Or Procuring Dd60
- DD64 Causing Or Permitting Dd60

- DD66 Inciting Dd60
- DD70 Causing Death By Reckless Driving
- DD72 Aiding, Abetting, Counselling Or Procuring Dd70
- DD74 Causing Or Permitting Dd70
- DD76 Inciting Dd70
- DD80 Causing Death By Dangerous Driving
- DD82 Aiding, Abetting, Counselling Or Procuring Dd80
- DD84 Causing Or Permitting Dd80
- DD86 Inciting Dd80

Drink or drugs: DR10, 20, 30 & 80: 3-11 Penalty Points. DR40, 50, 60 & 90: 10 Penalty Points. DR70: 4 Penalty Points.

- DR10 To Attempt Or Drive With Blood Alcohol Above Limit
- DR12 Aiding, Abetting, Counselling Or Procuring Dr10
- DR14 Causing Or Permitting Dr10
- R22 Aiding, Abetting, Counselling Or Procuring Dr20
- DR24 Causing Or Permitting Dr20
- DR26 Inciting Dr20
- DR30 To Attempt Or Drive Then Refuse Blood/Urine Test
- DR32 Aiding, Abetting, Counselling Or Procuring Dr30
- DR34 Causing Or Permitting Dr30
- DR36 Inciting Dr30
- DR40 In Charge Of Veh. With Blood Alcohol Above Limit
- DR42 Aiding, Abetting, Counselling Or Procuring Dr40
- DR44 Causing Or Permitting Dr40
- DR46 Inciting Dr40
- DR50 In Charge Of Veh. While Unfit Through Drink/Drugs
- DR52 Aiding, Abetting, Counselling Or Procuring Dr50
- DR54 Causing Or Permitting Dr50
- DR56 Inciting Dr50

- DR60 In Charge Of Veh. Then Refuse Blood/Urine Test
- DR62 Aiding, Abetting, Counselling Or Procuring Dr60DR16 Inciting Dr10
- DR20 To Attempt Or Drive While Unfit Through Drink/Drug
- DR64 Causing Or Permitting Dr60
- DR66 Inciting Dr60
- DR70 Failing To Provide Specimen For Breath Test
- DR72 Aiding, Abetting, Counselling Or Procuring Dr70
- DR74 Causing Or Permitting Dr70
- DR76 Inciting Dr70
- DR80 Driving Or Attempting To When Unfit Through Drugs
- DR82 Aiding, Abetting, Counselling Or Procuring Dr80
- DR84 Causing Or Permitting Dr80
- DR86 Inciting Dr80
- DR90 In Charge Of A Vehicle When Unfit Through Drugs
- DR92 Aiding, Abetting, Counselling Or Procuring Dr90
- DR94 Causing Or Permitting Dr90
- DR96 Inciting Dr90

Insurance offences: IN10: 6-8 Penalty Points.

- IN10 Using A Veh. Uninsured Against Third Party Risks
- IN12 Aiding, Abetting, Counselling Or Procuring In10
- IN14 Causing Or Permitting In10
- IN16 Inciting In10

Licence offences: LC20, 30, 40 & 50: 3-6 Penalty Points.

- LC10 Driving Without A Licence
- LC12 Aiding, Abetting, Counselling Or Procuring Lc10
- LC14 Causing Or Permitting Lc10
- LC16 Inciting Lc10
- LC20 Driving Otherwise Than In Accordance With A Lic

- LC22 Aiding, Abetting, Counselling Or Procuring Lc20
- LC24 Causing Or Permitting Lc20
- LC26 Inciting Lc20
- LC30 False Health Declaration When Applying For Licence
- LC32 Aiding, Abetting, Counselling Or Procuring Lc30
- LC34 Causing Or Permitting Lc30
- LC36 Inciting Lc30
- LC40 Driving A Vehicle Having Failed To Notify A Disability
- LC42 Aiding, Abetting, Counselling Or Procuring Lc40
- LC44 Causing Or Permitting Lc40
- LC46 Inciting Lc40
- LC50 Driving After Licence Has Been Revoked For Health
- LC52 Aiding, Abetting, Counselling Or Procuring Lc50
- LC54 Causing Or Permitting Lc50
- LC56 Inciting Lc50

Miscellaneous offences: MS10, 20, 70 & 80: 3 Penalty Points. MS30: 2 Penalty Points. MS50: 3-11 Penalty Points. MS60: As appropriate. MS90: 6 Penalty Points.

- MS10 Leaving A Veh. In A Dangerous Position
- MS12 Aiding, Abetting, Counselling Or Procuring Ms10
- MS14 Causing Or Permitting Ms10
- MS16 Inciting Ms10
- MS20 Unlawful Pillion Riding
- MS22 Aiding, Abetting, Counselling Or Procuring Ms20
- MS24 Causing Or Permitting
- MS26 Inciting Ms20
- MS30 Playstreet Offences
- MS32 Aiding, Abetting, Counselling Or Procuring Ms30
- MS34 Causing Or Permitting Ms30

- MS36 Inciting Ms30
- MS40 Drive With Uncorrected Eyesight Or Refuse Test
- MS42 Aiding, Abetting, Counselling Or Procuring Ms40
- MS44 Causing Or Permitting Ms40
- MS46 Inciting Ms40
- MS50 Motor Racing On The Highway
- MS52 Aiding, Abetting, Counselling Or Procuring Ms50
- MS54 Causing Or Permitting Ms50
- MS56 Inciting Ms50
- MS60 Offences Not Covered By Other Codes
- MS62 Aiding, Abetting, Counselling Or Procuring Ms60
- MS64 Causing Or Permitting Ms60
- MS66 Inciting Ms60
- MS70 Driving With Uncorrected Defective Eyesight
- MS72 Aiding, Abetting, Counselling Or Procuring Ms70
- MS74 Causing Or Permitting Ms70
- MS76 Inciting Ms70
- MS80 Refusing To Submit To An Eyesight Test
- MS82 Aiding, Abetting, Counselling Or Procuring Ms80
- MS84 Causing Or Permitting Ms80
- MS86 Inciting Ms80
- MS90 Failure To Give Info As To Identity Of Driver Etc
- MS92 Aiding, Abetting, Counselling Or Procuring Ms90
- MS94 Causing Or Permitting Ms90
- MS96 Inciting Ms90

Motorway offences: MW10: 3 Penalty Points.
- MW10 Disobey Special Road Regulations (Ex. Speed Limit)
- MW12 Aiding, Abetting, Counselling Or Procuring Mw10
- MW14 Causing Or Permitting Mw10

- MW16 Inciting Mw10

Pedestrian crossings: PC10, 20 & 30: 3 Penalty Points.

- PC10 Undefined Contravention Of Pedestrian Crossing
- PC12 Aiding, Abetting, Counselling Or Procuring Pc10
- PC14 Causing Or Permitting Pc10
- PC16 Inciting Pc10
- PC20 Contravention Of Ped/Crossing With Moving Vehicle
- PC22 Aiding, Abetting, Counselling Or Procuring Pc20
- PC24 Causing Or Permitting Pc20
- PC26 Inciting Pc20
- PC30 Contravention Of Ped/Crossing With Stationary Veh.
- PC32 Aiding, Abetting, Counselling Or Procuring Pc30
- PC34 Causing Or Permitting Pc30
- PC36 Inciting Pc30

Speed limits: SP10, 20, 30, 40 & 50: 3-6 Penalty Points.

Automatic for regulated "speed traps":

- Limit + up to 14 mph - 3 Penalty Points
- Limit + 15 - 19 mph - 4 Penalty Points
- Limit + 20 - 24 mph - 5 Penalty Points
- Limit + 25 - 29 mph - 6 Penalty Points
- SP10 Exceeding Goods Vehicle Speed Limit
- SP12 Aiding, Abetting, Counselling Or Procuring Sp10
- SP14 Causing Or Permitting Sp10
- SP16 Inciting Sp10
- SP20 Exceed Speed For Type Of Veh (Ex Goods/Passenger)
- SP22 Aiding, Abetting, Counselling Or Procuring Sp20
- SP24 Causing Or Permitting Sp20
- SP26 Inciting Sp20

- SP30 Exceeding Speed Limit On A Public Road
- SP32 Aiding, Abetting, Counselling Or Procuring Sp30
- SP34 Causing Or Permitting Sp30
- SP36 Inciting Sp30
- SP40 Exceeding Passenger Vehicle Speed Limit
- SP42 Aiding, Abetting, Counselling Or Procuring Sp40
- SP44 Causing Or Permitting Sp40
- SP46 Inciting Sp40
- SP50 Exceeding Speed Limit On A Motorway
- SP52 Aiding, Abetting, Counselling Or Procuring Sp50
- SP54 Causing Or Permitting Sp50
- SP56 Inciting Sp50
- SP60 Undefined Speed Limit Offence
- SP62 Aiding, Abetting, Counselling Or Procuring Sp60
- SP66 Inciting Sp60

Traffic direction and signs: TS10, 20, 30, 40, 50, 60 & 70: 3 Penalty Points

- TS10 Failing To Comply With Traffic Light Signals
- TS12 Aiding, Abetting, Counselling Or Procuring Ts10
- TS14 Causing Or Permitting Ts10
- TS16 Inciting Ts10
- TS20 Failing To Comply With Double White Lines
- TS22 Aiding, Abetting, Counselling Or Procuring Ts20
- TS24 Causing Or Permitting Ts20
- TS26 Inciting Ts20
- TS30 Failing To Comply With A Stop" Sign
- TS32 Aiding, Abetting, Counselling Or Procuring Ts30
- TS34 Causing Or Permitting Ts30
- TS36 Inciting Ts30
- TS40 Failing To Comply With Directions Of Traff/Police

- TS42 Aiding, Abetting, Counselling Or Procuring Ts40
- TS44 Causing Or Permitting Ts40
- TS46 Inciting Ts40
- TS50 Fail To Traff/Sign Ex Stop,Traff/Light,Dble W/Line
- TS52 Aiding, Abetting, Counselling Or Procuring Ts50
- TS54 Causing Or Permitting Ts50
- TS56 Inciting Ts50
- TS60 Failing To Comply With School Crossing Patrol Sign
- TS62 Aiding, Abetting, Counselling Or Procuring Ts60
- TS64 Causing Or Permitting Ts60
- TS66 Inciting Ts60
- TS70 Failure To Comply With Traffic Direction Or Sign
- TS72 Aiding, Abetting, Counselling Or Procuring Ts70
- TS74 Causing Or Permitting Ts70
- TS76 Inciting Ts70

Special code
* TT99 Disqualification Under The "Totting Up" Procedure

Theft or unauthorised taking: UT50: 3-11 Penalty Points.

- UT10 Take/Drive Away Vehicle Without Consent Or Attempt
- UT12 Aiding, Abetting, Counselling Or Procuring Ut10
- UT14 Causing Or Permitting Ut10
- UT16 Inciting Ut10
- UT20 Stealing Or Attempting To Steal A Vehicle
- UT22 Aiding, Abetting, Counselling Or Procuring Ut20
- UT24 Causing Or Permitting Ut20
- UT26 Inciting Ut20
- UT30 Going Equipped For Stealing Or Taking A Vehicle
- UT32 Aiding, Abetting, Counselling Or Procuring Ut30

- UT34 Causing Or Permitting Ut30
- UT36 Inciting Ut30
- UT40 Take/Drive (Attempt);Carried In;Veh W/Out Consent
- UT42 Aiding, Abetting, Counselling Or Procuring Ut40
- UT44 Causing Or Permitting Ut40
- UT46 Inciting Ut40
- UT50 Aggravated Taking Of A Vehicle
- UT52 Aiding, Abetting, Counselling Or Procuring Ut50
- UT54 Causing Or Permitting Ut50
- UT56 Inciting Ut50

Let us just go over again the offence procedure for all drivers, commercial and private. The law states for most motoring offences you shall not be prosecuted unless:-

- you have been warned at the time by a police officer, or
- you have been charged or served with a summons within 14 days, or
- a notice of intended prosecution has been sent to you or to the registered keeper of the vehicle within fourteen days

If you receive a notice of intended prosecution through the post, you could also receive a notice asking you to identify the driver. Unless you have a reasonable excuse, failure to supply the information would make you liable to a penalty similar to the alleged offence itself, i.e. a fine and penalty points. It is now common for speeding prosecutions to be based on photographic evidence.

However, there are exceptions to these principles, for example:-

- if the alleged offence relates to a road traffic accident, no notice of intended prosecution is required

- many parking offences do not require a notice of intended prosecution

It is advisable to take expert legal advice if you have any doubts in this area. Any 'ticket' concerning a motoring offence should be dealt with quickly. If you delay or ignore them things will only get worse, because you can end up having to pay more and or lose the right to dispute matters.

The three types of 'ticket' are:-

- Penalty Charge Notice
- Fixed Penalty Notice
- Conditional Offer Notice

Generally the more serious motoring offences are dealt with in the Magistrates' Court in England and Wales or the Sheriff's Court in Scotland. Once a summons is issued you have two options:-

- Plead guilty. This can either be done by post or in person. However, if the Court is considering a ban (this will depend on the offence or how many penalty points you already have) you will need to attend the Court.
- Plead not guilty. We have covered this subject and will be looking at it further in the book. You may consider seeking legal advice if you plan to take this option.

If you are in any doubt as to what to do, seek expert legal advice. It is impossible to state exactly what penalty a court may impose, but individual advice may be able to give some general indication of the possible sentence.

Generally, it is rare for the maximum penalty to be imposed. The courts take into account:-

- the seriousness of the offence
- any mitigating circumstances relating to the offence or the defendant
- previous convictions
- the defendant's means

You can be asked for your financial details and may have to complete a Means Enquiry Form. A Magistrate's Court in England or Wales, having assessed the offence, can lower or raise the fine if felt appropriate given your means. In Scotland, the court will take into account the seriousness of the offence and may consider a defendant's means if there is an application for time to pay.

TWO

SPEEDING AND SPEED LIMITS

Do you speed, perhaps to make up for lost time on your journey? To get home faster when you are running late? You are not alone.

Here is a police statement on speeding:-

> *"Despite the frightening casualty figures, surveys continue to show that almost all drivers and riders exceed speed limits at some time.*
>
> *A survey in 1998 showed that in free flowing traffic –*
>
> - *69% of cars exceeded the 30 mph limit*
> - *29% exceeded the 40 mph limit*
>
> *Speeding is endemic. It is socially acceptable, and we almost all do it. "*

That suggested almost two thirds of motorists, private and professional , speed on a regular basis. It means that on a regular basis, your licence is at risk.

If you are booked for speeding as a result of a fixed radar speed camera, typically the GATSO type of camera, there are several options open to you. There is a problem with GATSO cameras, namely that the radars that activate the camera sequence use the speed recorded by the radar. They therefore only look at one photograph in order to obtain the registration number of the target vehicle. If you think this is incorrect, you should follow this procedure.

In cases where you are uncertain whether you have been speeding, you should have been sent or will need to ask for a copy of both the photographs that were taken of you by the camera. You should also ask about the time delay, how far apart in time the pictures were actually taken. The police are legally required to forward you the photos. Look at the lines that are painted on the road and you can see how far you have travelled in the time it took to take both pictures , normally the pictures are taken a half second apart. Go to the camera site and carefully measure the distance between these lines. Now you know how far your car or truck moved in that time period.

You can then calculate your speed and if it is the speed you have been notified of – it's a fair cop!

There are a number of other factors that need to be taken into account when considering the accuracy of a speed camera. The police officer should be fully trained in the use of the camera equipment, and can only operate it on foot. Speed cameras may not be operated from a vehicle. In general, the camera should be positioned in such a way that it is clearly visible to oncoming vehicles. It is also a recommendation that the speed detection device should only be used where the police officer has reasonable grounds to believe that the vehicle he is aiming it at may be exceeding the speed limit. The officer should point the speed gun directly at the approaching vehicle, keeping it parallel and holding it steady for at least three seconds. The officer then presses a button or trader on the gun and the reading is recorded in the device.

Radar speed cameras are required to be professionally checked and calibrated at least once a year. Before the police officer uses the device they should check it against the speedometer of the police vehicle they are using and should repeat of this check after they have completed using the device. They are then required to record that this check has been done and the results of the check in the police officer's notebook. Failure to carry out any of these procedures does not in itself guarantee that a case of speeding will be overturned, but it is extremely good grounds for stating your case.

Laser speed guns are the latest weapon in the police force's speed detection equipment. The device is known as laser infrared detection and ranging device. In theory laser speed guns can be used with much greater precision than a conventional radar gun and in addition they are subject to less interference than radar guns. However these laser guns do need to be aimed very accurately at the target vehicle. Once again, the police officer operating the gun needs to be technically trained and competent in the use of the device and should be able to produce evidence to this effect. Failure to be able was to support this kind of training could well result in your case being acquitted. In addition laser guns can only be used  during daylight hours and cannot be used through the windscreen of police car. If you are booked for speeding when such a device has been used you should check that the police officers concerned have taken all of these steps with regard to training and calibration. If they have not, you have a very good chance of being acquitted.

Visual average speed computer and recorder is that less sophisticated and generally regarded as more accurate device for measuring speed. Essentially, the police officer presses a button as the vehicle passes a

53

reference point and the device begins timing. As the vehicle passed the second reference point the officer presses the button again and by measuring the time taken for the vehicle to travel between the two points the speed of the vehicle can be checked. However, use of these devices is not entirely straightforward and police officers need to be extremely well trained in their use and to have a high standard of visual skill. They should be able to demonstrate that their ability in respect of the use of this kind of device has been thoroughly tested and approved. Once again, the device needs to be checked and calibrated at least once a year and a certificate issued to this effect. If you are accused of a speeding offence using this type of device, or indeed any other speed testing device, you should make sure that you request all of the relevant documentation with regard to testing, calibration and training of the operating officer.

Pacing is another method that police used to check vehicles speed. In this method of the police vehicle, car or motorcycle, will follow your van or lorry for a certain distance and will keep pace with your vehicle. This needs to be done is for a minimum distance of a quarter of a mile. At no time during the pacing process should any other vehicle come between the police vehicle and your vehicle, and if this does occur this it is grounds to have an offence set aside. It is essential that the police vehicle using this method of speed checking has a speedometer that has been properly checked and calibrated.

Police officers are in fact required to record and check that their speedometer has been calibrated both before and after using it for this purpose, noting this in their police notebook. If you are accused of speeding using the pacing system, you should obtain the police records both of calibration of the vehicle speedometer and of the records in the police notebook, both before and after it was used. Although traffic police vehicles have a speedometer that is more than likely to have followed this procedure, other police patrol cars do not have more accurate types of calibrated speedometers. If and when you are stopped for speeding ask the police officer for details of their speedometer calibration, with times, dates and results. It is entirely possible that the officer will not pursue the offence.

Lately we have seen a number of fixed position cameras installed, whereby the cameras are set in pairs a given distance apart. The first camera will record the vehicle's number plate as it passes, the second camera will make a similar record and compare the time and distance travelled with the data from the first camera. In this way the equipment can determine whether or not the vehicle was speeding. These new cameras are generally highly visible and the best defence against them is to keep a wary eye out for this kind of device. They are often painted yellow. Should you be unlucky enough to be accused of speeding as a result of this equipment, either by a police car that follows you and flags you down after the offence has been committed or perhaps by way of a letter through the post, the defence is very difficult. Once again the best fall-back is to require full details of the equipment's tests and calibration certificates, together with the details of the approved training of the police and civilians who have operated the equipment.

There are a number of practical steps you can take to protect yourself from speeding offences. If you search the internet there are several websites that have a list of locations of speed cameras, these will help you to keep an eye out for fixed speed camera installations. Some people suggest that is obscuring your number plate, by the use of so-called invisible number plate technology. This is of course illegal and the police are well aware of this trick. If you are caught doing it as a professional driver the likelihood is that the penalty will be considerably more onus than that for the speeding offence itself that you were trying to avoid, so give this kind of equipment and miss.

On board radar detection equipment can be useful, though not infallible. The best types of systems will have programmed into them the locations of all of the fixed speed cameras together with updated camera positions as they become known. You should bear in mind that these will not help you whatsoever against many mobile speed cameras and relying on this kind of equipment is only helpful. It is not a complete solution in itself.

Should you actually be accused of an offence of speeding the police are required to issue a notice of intended prosecution through the post. The law states that this notice must be served within fourteen days of the alleged offence. If the police failed to issue the notice to you in this time it is invalid. Should you receive one of these notices check the times and dates at very carefully, this could be a complete defence in itself. Note that the fourteen day period does not necessarily take into account the time that the notice took to reach you, it is only the time in which the police are required to issue the notice from the actual time of the offence. The notice will be issued to the owner of the vehicle or the registered keeper, should the actual driver be unknown. The keeper is then required by law to notify the police as to who was driving their vehicle at the time the offence was committed. Once you have a notice of intended prosecution you are required to reply to this within twenty eight days. In your reply you can either accept you were guilty of the offence and pay the fine that is proposed, or you can refuse and deny the offence, in this case is the matter will be dealt with by the court, usually a magistrate's court. If you already have a number of points on your driving licence, and your livelihood is a risk, you would be well advised to employ it a good solicitor in this case and co-operate with them to produce a viable defence. You should go back and check the circumstances of the offence, to see if there are any reasons for cameras returning a false signal. If your vehicle is excessively large it has been known that these can produce false readings if the vehicle is vibrating excessively, or causing objects at the roadside to vibrate excessively.

Even a car stereo played very loudly can cause a speed camera to produce a false reading. As we stated previously, you need to collect and gather all of the information possible, including the photographs from the speed camera and all of the documents and certification, to confirm the accuracy of the camera and of its operator. Sometimes, cameras take a picture when the car passes that is supposed to give some identification of the driver, that this is not always conclusive and occasionally cases have been thrown out where the driver cannot be accurately identified. It is unmistakably you? This could be a useful defence used to mount.

Yet another useful defence that can be used is where the camera was sited according to the relevant parameters.

These parameters are:-

- The camera should on a site of between 400m and 1500m in length.

- There should be at least three fatal or near fatal accidents in three years prior to the offence.

- A determination is made of the speed at which 85% of vehicles travel on the particular stretch of road, and the recorded speech should be greater than this.

- Cameras should only be sited where at least 20% of drivers exceed the speed limit.

- Camera should only be sited where other methods to reduce vehicle speed cannot be used, for example speed bumps.

All of these factors are worth checking should you be booked for speeding, and if any of them have not been met you have good grounds to defend your case. In general cameras should be highly visible, normally coloured yellow. However, this is not an absolute role so that do not depend on it for your defence. On the other hand, the deliberate hiding or obscuring of the camera with a fixed or mobile behind a tree or bush is categorically not allowed. If in fact the camera has recorded you as speeding at night on an unlit road this is also a good grounds to defend your case, as clearly a speed check camera on an unlit road is in no way highly visible.

Here are the ACPO guidelines for speeding. This will indicate exactly what you, as a professional driver, are up against when you are on the road. Speeding constitutes the commonest offence for the truck and van driver:

The enforcement of traffic law by the police should be guided by the principles of proportionality in applying the law and securing compliance; targeting of enforcement action; consistency of approach; and transparency about what enforcement action is undertaken, and why; and recognition that effective partnerships with other organisations are essential.

Proportionality means relating enforcement action to the risks. Those whom the law protects and those on whom it places duties expect that action taken by the police to achieve compliance (in this case speed limits) should be proportionate to the risks to individuals and property and to the seriousness of any breach.

Targeting means making sure that enforcement action is directed primarily at those whose behaviour poses the greatest risk (particularly to others), often at identifiable locations or in identifiable circumstances. Targeting needs to take full advantage of a wide range of information sources, including academic research, to develop a greater level of understanding of what the problems are and how to resolve them, so that enforcement action can be focused and prioritised.   Effective targeting will therefore ensure that road risks are objectively identified and prioritised for appropriate action; that suitable resources are deployed; and that pertinent monitoring and evaluation takes place so that costs and benefits can be properly assessed and future decision making enhanced.

Consistency of approach does not mean uniformity. It does mean taking a similar approach in similar circumstances to achieve similar ends. Police officers are faced with many variables; the decision as to what action to take is a matter of judgement, and they must exercise their discretion.

Where Police Officers believe that an offence has been committed (in this case, that a motorist has driven at any speed over the relevant speed limit), in exercising their discretion as to the appropriate enforcement action, they must consider the nature and circumstances of the offence. Depending on those circumstances they may decide to issue a summons, issue a fixed penalty notice, caution, warn or take no action. For instance, it might be appropriate to issue a summons for exceeding a speed limit at relatively low speeds over the relevant limit on roads near schools at certain times of day or when there are adverse weather conditions, whereas a similar offence committed in the middle of the night might merit the issue of a fixed penalty notice.

Road users do expect consistency from the police nationally, and this feature has been identified as a benefit linked to the operation of speed cameras.   Inconsistency in enforcement practice undermines public confidence and contributes to resentment. It is part of ACPO's role to ensure that consistency is achieved wherever possible.

Transparency means helping drivers to understand what is expected of them and why. It also means ensuring clarity about what the public can expect from the police. Raising the public's understanding of the full implications of their actions (specifically including the human and financial costs) will assist in changing behaviour and ultimately attitudes.

The way in which ACPO tries to achieve transparency is by publishing guidance to chief constables to enable them, in turn, to offer operational advice and guidance to their officers. ACPO's guidance is placed in the public domain. ACPO's guidance has been formulated having taken account of the need for proportionality (especially with the introduction of Human Rights legislation) and the need for targeting in order to maximise the potential of scarce police resources and make a substantial contribution to the multi-agency road death and injury reduction effort.

Driving at any speed over the limit is an offence. The differing speed limits are generally related, and proportionate, to the risks to all road users using that road. Where police officers consider that an offence has been committed i.e. that a motorist has driven at any speed over the relevant speed limit, they should consider whether it is appropriate to take enforcement action against the offender. The Police Service now uses technology that enables it to prove that an offence has been committed as soon as a driver exceeds the relevant speed limit by a very small margin. Motorists will therefore be at risk of prosecution immediately they exceed any legal speed limit. The guidance to police

officers is that it is anticipated that, other than in the most exceptional circumstances, the issue of fixed penalty notices and summonses is likely to be the minimum appropriate enforcement action as soon as the following speeds have been reached.

We made the last paragraph bold so that you could not miss it. For those professional drivers that travel across Europe, different rules to apply and you should check what is relevant for the country concerned.

Advisory/Mandatory Speed Limits on Motorways

Advisory speed limits on motorways are shown by illuminated signs and indicate hazardous situations and roadworks ahead. The amber flashing warning lights located on the nearside of motorways indicate danger ahead – you should slow down until the road is clear. Failure to observe these signs can lead to prosecution for offences such as "driving without due care." Mandatory limits may also be found on motorways at roadworks sites (indicated by a white sign with black letters and red border). Failure to comply with these particular signs can result in speeding prosecutions.

Remember, if you are accused of any speeding offence, you need to gather as much documentation and evidence as possible. The law is complicated, and the more you delve into the circumstances of your offence, the more likely you are to find that the police or CPS have erred in some way sufficiently to throw out the charge against you.

You need to record everything:-

- the officers collar number
- the time, date and place
- weather conditions
- traffic conditions
- visibility
- anything else that you could use to cast doubt on your accusers

You need the camera photos, if any, copies of calibration and testing of the equipment used, copies of officers notebook entries, copies confirming the officers completion of training on the type of equipment used. Does the notification have any errors with regard to date and time? Was the NIP issued within the required time frame of fourteen days. There are many, many areas in which police can make mistakes, they are, after all, only human. These mistakes can overturn the case against you, thousands of drivers have managed to do exactly that.

THREE

WHEEL CLAMPS AND PARKING

Firstly, let us start by taking a look at wheel clamps. There are two distinct types of wheel clamping:-

- on private ground
- on public areas, roads etc.

Wheel clampers used by private landowners must have a licence from the Security Industry Authority (SIA). It is a criminal offence for anyone without a licence to clamp your vehicle. It is also a criminal offence for someone to employ an unlicenced wheel clamper, or for a landowner to allow a wheel clamper who they know is unlicenced to operate on their property.

When you pay to have your vehicle released, the wheel clamper must provide a receipt which includes the following information: -

- the place where the vehicle was clamped
- their name and signature
- their SIA licence number (a 15 digit number on the front of their licence)
- the date

Licenced wheel clampers should also wear their SIA licence where you can see it at all times when they are working.

You can check whether someone has a valid SIA licence by looking on a public register of licences on the SIA website at:-

- www.the-sia.org.uk
- the SIA call centre on 08702 430 100

When can your vehicle be clamped?

If you park on private land without the owner's permission, they can legally clamp your vehicle. However, they can only do this under certain conditions.

Some examples of when your vehicle might be clamped on private land are when:-

- you have parked in a car park reserved for customers of a pub and you are not a customer
- you have parked in the car park of a block of flats, where you are not a resident
- you have parked in a car park reserved for employees of a company
- you have failed to display a ticket or permit properly
- you have parked across two spaces instead of one you have parked dangerously, or blocked an emergency access.

In order for your vehicle to be legally clamped there must be notices up:-

- where you can clearly see them
- warning that unauthorised vehicles will be clamped
- the landowner does not charge more than a reasonable fee to release your vehicle
- your vehicle is released as soon as you have said you will pay the release fee
- there is a way for you to get in touch with the landowner (or their agent) to make arrangements to pay, for example a telephone number on the warning notice.

It is a SIA requirement that a landowner must not clamp your vehicle if:-

- it displays a valid disabled badge
- it is a marked as an emergency service vehicle attending an emergency.

If you are clamped:-

- Keep calm, do not lose your temper or attempt to remove a wheel clamp - you could be sued for criminal damage if you damage the wheel-clamp. You could be also prosecuted for theft if you keep the clamp.
- Contact the telephone number shown and ask for release.
- Check whether warning signs and boundaries are clear enough. You could also take a photograph to use as evidence later on.
- Ask the wheel clamper who they work for, whether the landowners authority can be produced, and if they have a licence from the SIA.
- Ask to see the licence — it is your right as a clamped motorist.
- If you do not think a wheel clamper is licenced, do not pay the release fee. If they refuse to release your vehicle without a fee, call the police.

An unlicensed wheel-clamper is committing a criminal offence. Report unlicenced wheel clampers to the SIA. If the wheel clamper uses threatening or intimidating behaviour, you should report this to the police. If the wheel clamper is licenced you will have to pay the release fee, but insist on a receipt.

Try to get the address and phone number at which the wheel clamper can be contacted if you think you should not have been clamped, for example because the warning notices were inadequate, or the release fee was too high.

The only way to get your money back may be through the courts. A solicitor will be able to advise you on what chance you have of winning your case.

It may be necessary to tow away a vehicle parked on private land if it is:-

- dangerously parked
- causing an obstruction
- blocking an emergency access

If your vehicle is towed away from private land:-

- Look for any notices with contact information for the site owners or managers.
- If you are in London and you think your vehicle has been towed away, you can use the TRACE service to find out where it is (Tel: 020 7747 4747).
- Contact the local police station — they should be informed when a vehicle has been removed (do not dial 999 however!).
- You will have to pay to get the vehicle released, but you may want to get legal advice from a solicitor.

You can also look on the website of the British Parking Association which acts as a trade association for companies that carry out parking enforcement activities on private land. Members of the Association must comply with a Code of Practice on wheel clamping and vehicle removal.

Secondly, there is the issue of wheel clamping on public roads and areas, becoming more prevalent lately in the UK. The decision on whether to immobilise or to remove a vehicle requires an exercise of judgement and must only be taken following specific authorisation by an appropriately trained person. The immobilisation/removal operatives themselves should not take the decision.

Vehicles should not be immobilised or removed by contractors unless a suitably trained person is present to confirm that the contravention falls within the guidelines.

- When a vehicle is parked where parking is permitted, authorities must not immobilise or remove in the first 30 minutes following the issuing of the notice, with the exception of 'persistent evader' vehicles ... where the time limit is 15 minutes. When a vehicle has been immobilised, a person must affix a notice to it. The regulations set out what that notice must say. The immobilisation device may only be removed by or under the direction of a person authorised to do so by the enforcement authority, following payment of the release fee and the penalty charge.

- If a driver returns to the vehicle whilst immobilisation or removal is taking place, then unless they are a persistent evader, it is recommended that the operation is halted, unless the clamp is secured or the vehicle has all its wheels aboard the tow truck. If immobilisation or removal is halted the PCN should still be enforced.

- When a vehicle is immobilised and subsequently removed to the pound, the driver does not have to pay the clamp release fee.

- Where vehicles are removed, enforcement authorities should contact the police or, in London, TRACE and advise them of the time, place, vehicle registration number, and pound to attend for retrieval so they can deal with queries from motorists who report their vehicle stolen.

- Where a vehicle has been immobilised or removed, an authority should seek to make it available to its owner immediately upon payment. In the case of clamp release, enforcement authorities should set maximum times for releasing vehicles once they have received payment. They should publish these along with their parking policy guidelines. It is recommended that these should be within one hour from payment being received, with a maximum time limit of two hours. The immobilisation or removal is the penalty and further inconvenience and potential cost from prolonged release times is not appropriate. Enforcement authorities should publish their performance against these targets.

- On the release of a vehicle from a clamp or from the vehicle pound the authority must immediately inform the vehicle owner or person in charge of the vehicle about their right to make representations and their subsequent right to appeal against representations that are rejected. The vehicle will already have been issued a PCN that sets out the grounds on which representations can be made. However, the Secretary of State recommends that the notice about representations against the immobilisation or removal also gives full particulars of the grounds, procedure and time limit for representations. This is particularly important when credit or debit payments are made over the telephone.

Storage charges should apply for each day or part of day, reckoned from 2400 midnight on the day following removal of a vehicle.

In the event of your lorry or van being clamped, there are certain procedures that the clamper does need to follow. Parking in itself is not a criminal offence, but has become for many local authorities and indeed private landowners a major source of revenue.

Local authorities and police are required by law to observe the following procedures:=

- The vehicle needs to be issued with a notice that it is parked illegally and will be clamped.

- Where you return to your van or lorry before the padlock of the clamp is closed, the clamp must be removed.

- This also applies where you return to your vehicle before it is completely off the ground, again the clamp must be removed.

- If your vehicle is displaying a valid disabled driver badge, it should not be clamped.

- If your vehicle displays a badge stating it is being used for health emergency, it should not be clamped

- If your vehicle has been overdue for parking fees for less than 15 minutes, it should not be clamped.

If your truck is clamped, you will have to pay a penalty charge, the release fee, together with any storage charge if necessary before it will be released. In addition you will need to show some evidence that the vehicle does belong to you or is in your charge. After the clamp being removed the operator is required to give you a minimum of one hour to remove the vehicle before they can refix the clamp.

Should you wish to oppose the clamping, or at least the penalty charge that was imposed on you, on the basis that the clamping was unlawful, unfair or outside of the regulations as they applied the time, you will need to write to your local authority within twenty eight days. If you want to make a worthwhile case for the clamping fee to be waived, you will need to send substantial evidence to back your case. This could be by way of site drawings and maps, photographs, and statements from any witnesses if possible. The procedure then is that the council will either accept or reject your claim. If they do reject it you are entitled to take your case to the Appeal Court.

Private clampers are an entirely different matter. Their regulation is a very hit and miss affair and the charges that they make to release your vehicle can be very high indeed to the point of extortionate. As stated above, there is an authority that monitors the activities of clampers, the

SIA. Under the law, you are required to give notional consent of clamping by placing your vehicle in an area that is clearly marked as being an area where vehicles will be clamped if they contravene the regulations that apply to that particular area.

In practice, this means that the clamper has to display a sign that is extremely visible and unequivocally clear to the driver. Again, if you are going to appeal the clamping release fee you will need photos to back up your case to the court that the clamper did not give adequate warning of their activities and therefore you are unable to give your consent to the clamping. The law is a grey area, especially with regard to private clampers. The rule here is if in doubt, appeal the clampers and provide as much evidence as you are able to do. There is an ombudsman for all areas of England and Wales to whom you can apply for advice and possible action against the clamper. This is a route that can be well worth following.

Parking generally is an area that poses a number of problems for the professional driver and will frequently find them falling foul of the regulations.

Here is a general summary of the regulations as they apply across the UK:-

Clearways

The road sign indicating a clearway is circular, with a red diagonal cross on a blue background surrounded by a red circle. Vehicles must not stop (other than in an emergency) on the carriageway of a clearway or on the carriageway or verge of an urban clearway during the times shown on the sign, other than for as long as is necessary to let passengers board or alight.

Parking and Overtaking

Vehicles must not park or overtake other vehicles in areas where danger or obstruction may be caused, as follows:-

- in a "no parking" area
- on a clearway
- along side yellow lines
- where there are double white lines
- near a road junction
- near a bend
- near the brow of a hill
- near a humpback bridge
- near a level crossing
- near a bus stop
- near a school entrance
- near a pedestrian crossing
- on the right-hand side of the road at night
- where the vehicle would obscure a traffic sign
- on a narrow road
- On fast main roads and motorways
- near entrances and exits used by emergency service vehicles (or by fire hydrants)
- near road works
- alongside or opposite another parked vehicle
- in a parking disc zone unless the vehicle displays a parking disc
- in a meter zone unless the meter fee has been paid
- at bus stops
- on a pavement or cycle track
- on flyovers
- in tunnels or in underpasses

The police can request a driver to remove a vehicle causing danger or obstruction or can forcibly remove it themselves and can prosecute the driver/registered owner.

Parking on Pedestrian Crossings

A vehicle must not be parked within the area marked by zigzag lines on either side of a zebra crossing or in the zone indicated by metal studs on the approach to a pedestrian crossing. Overtaking is also prohibited in these areas.

Night Parking

Vehicles parked on roads overnight must stand on the nearside except when parked in a one-way street or in a recognised parking place. Goods vehicles over 1,525kg unladen must always display lights when parked on roads at night. Goods vehicles not exceeding 1,525kg unladen may park without lights on roads where a speed limit is in force (restricted roads) provided they are facing the direction of travel (nearside to the kerb) and are not parked within 10 metres (15 yards in Northern Ireland) of a road junction on either side of the road. Trailers detached from the towing vehicle and vehicles carrying projecting loads must not be parked on roads at night without lights (detached trailers should never be parked on roads or in lay-bys, which are part of the highway). All parked vehicles must display lights at night when parked on roads where no speed limit is in force.

Loading and Unloading

Vehicles may be loaded and unloaded anywhere except where signs indicating the contrary. In some areas loading/unloading restrictions are indicated by yellow lines painted on the kerb at right angles (with relevant times given on nearby plates) as follows:-

- single yellow right angle lines indicate loading/unloading restrictions at the times shown on the nearby sign
- double yellow right angle lines indicate loading/unloading restrictions at all times

Loading and unloading in parking meter zones is not allowed during working hours except where a free meter space is available or there is a gap between meter areas. When using a meter bay for loading the meter fee does not have to be paid if the stopping time is 20 minutes or less. When stopping to load and unload and when leaving the vehicle unattended the engine must be stopped unless it is used for running auxiliary equipment.

Waiting Restrictions.

Yellow lines painted on the road parallel to the kerb indicate bans on waiting as follows:-

- a complete ban is shown by double yellow parallel lines
- a partial ban is shown by a single continuous yellow parallel line

In every case it is essential to consult the nearby sign (usually on a lamp post or wall) indicating the ban to see the precise times when it is in operation.

If you fall foul of the parking regulations a local authority may well these days issue a parking charge notice. The parking charge notice can also be issued by a company acting as an agent for the local authority. The parking charge notice is not supported by magistrate's court action if you fail to pay. Instead, failure to pay will mean that you may be taken to the county court for pursuit of payment of the debt.

These particular notices are always worth challenging, and once again it is essential that you gather as much evidence as possible to support your case, by way of plans and drawings, photos and if possible statements from witnesses. The whole area of parking charge notices is fairly complicated and in many ways quite a grey area and if you mount a competent challenge to a parking charge notice you do stand an extremely good chance of winning.

Should you be issued a more regular parking ticket by a traffic warden or similar, or a police officer, you would be well advised to keep notes of actually what happens as you are being handed the notice. You should make it clear to this person that you thought you were acting reasonably in parking where you were and you should request that the officer concerned makes a note of your comments.

Again, the more evidence that you can gather, the stronger case you can present when defending your case. You should reply to the parking ticket within fourteen days and enclose all of the evidence that you have available to you. You do have a good chance of winning your defence, depending on how strong the defence you can mount, how clear and complete is the evidence you provide in support and how strong the case is against you.

Should you lose the appeal there are further steps you can take but these are fraught with fine legal points and often not worth the time, expense and bother of mounting them. If you do wish to go down this road, you would be well advised to consult a solicitor with specific knowledge and experience of motoring cases.

Useful terms

Here is a handy list of terms that relate to parking and parking appeals. Knowing the jargon can often be half of the battle.

Additional Parking Charges

Penalty charges, charges made by London authorities for the removal, storage and disposal of vehicles and charges in respect of the release of vehicles from immobilisation devices fixed under section 69 of the Road Traffic Act 1991.

Appeal

The second and final statutory opportunity for a motorist to contest a civil traffic penalty through an appeal to an independent Adjudicator. The decision of an Adjudicator is final and binding on both parties to an appeal. A motorist may only appeal after the authority which issued the Penalty Charge Notice has rejected a formal representation and appeals may only made on certain, specified grounds.

Certificated Bailiff

A bailiff authorised by the County Court to recover civil traffic debts.

Charge Certificate

A notice issued to motorists who have not paid a penalty charge within the statutory time limits. A Charge Certificate increases the full penalty charge by 50%. If the penalty is not then paid within fourteen days the local authority may enforce payment as a debt in the County Court.

Contravention

A failure by a motorist to comply with traffic or parking controls.

Controlled Parking Zone (CPZ)

A zone for which the parking restrictions are shown by signs placed on all vehicular entry points to the zone. Within the zone, signs are only required where the restrictions are different from those on the entry signs. There will usually be no sign for a yellow line where the restrictions are the same as on the entry signs.

Costs

A Parking Adjudicator has only limited powers to award costs against either party to an appeal. The grounds for doing so are few and such awards are extremely rare. Costs may be awarded if in the opinion of the Adjudicator either party has behaved frivolously, vexatiously or wholly unreasonably.

County Court

The court where a debt may be registered following non payment of a Penalty Charge Notice fourteen days after the service of a Charge Certificate. Such debts are registered at the Traffic Enforcement Centre, currently attached to Northampton County Court.

Debt Registration

The process of recording a parking debt with the Traffic Enforcement Centre at the County Court, no fewer than fourteen days after the service of a Charge Certificate and where the penalty charge due has not been paid.

Decriminalisation

Under the Road Traffic Act 1991 the Secretary of State for Transport can make Special Parking Orders, permitting an authority to enforce contraventions of parking controls within a designated Special Parking Area. Such contraventions are not criminal offences, but are enforced through civil procedures. Thus they are said to have been "decriminalised".

Designated Parking Bays

Bays designated by means of a Traffic Management Order for specified types of parking, e.g. free parking, meter parking, resident permit or disabled badge holder parking. These are usually denoted by white boxes on the carriageway.

Discount Rate

Term often used to describe the reduced penalty.

Dispensation

An agreement to allow a vehicle to park in a restricted area, without penalty, for an agreed duration and without the need to pay any initial parking charge. Dispensations are issued by or on behalf of the authority and an administrative charge may be made for this service. Dispensations are typically granted in limited circumstances where alternative provision cannot be made, for example to enable works to take place at adjacent premises or for essential deliveries which will take longer than the maximum time permitted.

DVLA

Driver and Vehicle Licensing Agency, based in Swansea.

Enforcement Notice

A statutory notice to be served by the authority on the person believed by them to be the owner of a vehicle issued with a Penalty Charge Notice for a bus lane contravention where the penalty remains unpaid after twenty eight days. The Enforcement Notice requires the owner within twenty eight days to either;

    i)   make payment of the full penalty charge, or;

    ii) make representations against liability for the charge.

Exemptions

Various restrictions have exemptions, for example loading, unloading and the picking up and setting down of passengers and their luggage. Certain classes of vehicle may be granted exemption from traffic restrictions and parking controls, some by statute, for example statutory undertakers when on operational duties and others as detailed in a local authority's Traffic Management Orders, for example Post Office vehicles and removal lorries.

Fixed Penalty Notice (FPN)

Notices issued by police officers and police traffic wardens to motorists committing parking offences governed by criminal law.

Grounds

The relevant legislation details the legal grounds on which representations against liability for a penalty may be made. These are the same grounds on which an Adjudicator may consider an appeal against an authority's rejection of these initial representations.

Hand Held Computer (HHC)

A small, hand held computer that can be used to register parking contraventions and to print the subsequent Penalty Charge Notice. The HHC may contain an integral printer and also digital camera and even sound recording capabilities.

Hand Held Ticketing Terminal (HHTT)

Another name for a hand held computer. (See above).

Hire Vehicles

If a vehicle is hired under an agreement which conforms to The Road Traffic (Owner Liability) Regulations 2000 for less than six months and the hirer has signed a statement of liability for penalty charges, liability for any penalty charge may be transferred from the hire company, as the owner of the vehicle, to the hirer of the vehicle. This does not apply to bus lane contraventions.

Initial charge

The basic charge set for parking in a designated parking bay, for specified users at specified times. Individual councils have responsibility for setting their own initial charges.

Loading bay

A specific bay, bounded by white markings and signed to permit loading and unloading by goods vehicles. Parking is not permitted within these bays.

Loading gap

An area of yellow line between two bays. As with other yellow lines, waiting is restricted but the normal loading and unloading exemption applies.

London Local Authorities

The 33 London boroughs and Transport for London.

Notice of Acceptance

A notice issued by an authority to a motorist following their representations indicating that these have been accepted.

Notice of Rejection (NOR)

A notice issued by an authority to a motorist following their representations indicating that these have been rejected.

Notice to Owner (NTO)

A statutory notice to be served by the authority on the person believed by them to be the owner of a vehicle issued with a Penalty Charge Notice for a parking contravention where the penalty remains unpaid after twenty eight days. The Notice to Owner requires the owner within twenty eight days to either;

    i)   make payment of the full penalty charge, or;

    ii)   make representations against liability for the charge.

Notice of Appeal (NOA)

The appellant starts an appeal by sending a Notice of Appeal to PATAS. The Adjudicators have provided a standard form of Notice of Appeal which it is convenient to use for this purpose. This form should be issued by the local authority with each Notice of Rejection.

Offence

Term used to describe a breach of the criminal law. In decriminalised enforcement the term "contravention" and not "offence" should be used.

Order for recovery

County Court order for recovery of an unpaid penalty charge which has been registered as a debt at the Traffic Enforcement Centre.

Owner liability

The owner is generally liable for penalty charges, whoever was driving. There are exceptions, see Owner Liability. Owner liability does not apply to the London lorry ban, where both the operator and driver are liable.

Parking and Traffic Adjudicator

Parking and Traffic Adjudicators are judicial office holders, appointed under Traffic Management Act 2004. They must be barristers or solicitors of at least five years standing.

Parking Attendant (PA)

A designation given by the Road Traffic Act 1991 to those officers engaged by councils to issue Penalty Charge Notices. PAs may be employed direct by the council or through a specialist contractor.

Parking Bay

Sometimes used as an alternative for 'parking space'.

Parking Place

An area of highway designated within a Traffic Management Order as a place where vehicles may be parked. Sometimes used as an alternative for 'Designated parking bay' (see above).

Parking Space

A space for one vehicle within a designated parking bay.

Parking and Traffic Appeals Service (PATAS)

The name given to the administrative support provided for the London Adjudicators.

Penalty Charge Notice

A notice issued in respect of a vehicle alleging a contravention. A Penalty Charge Notice must contain certain information, including a description of which contravention is alleged to have occurred.

Personal Hearing

A motorist requesting a personal hearing should attend at the time and day set out in the notification letter. PATAS tries to give everyone their first choice of hearing time but if this would mean a long delay before a case is heard, it may be necessary to give another time. If the time arranged for a personal hearing is particularly inconvenient, PATAS will try to re-arrange it upon request.

Pocket Book

A notebook used by Parking Attendants to record information while on duty, including information about contraventions, to support Penalty Charge Notices issued during the course of their enforcement activities.

Postal decision

If the parties agree to a postal decision, the Adjudicator will decide the appeal on the papers only, without a personal hearing.

Pound

A secure place to which a removed vehicle is taken for storage until it is retrieved by the owner upon payment of the additional parking charges.

Priority Routes (red routes)

A network of major roads within London, specified by the Secretary of State as key roads where traffic flow is to be maintained.

Reduced Penalty

A reduction of 50% in the penalty charge if it is paid so that it is received by the local authority within fourteen days of the date of the Penalty Charge Notice. If you write within fourteen days to informally challenge a Penalty Charge Notice, some authorities will extend the fourteen days for paying the reduced penalty whilst considering your letter. But you should check with them whether they will do this as not all authorities do.

Registered Keeper

The person or organisation recorded at the Driver and Vehicle Licensing Agency as being the keeper of a vehicle. Under the concept of "owner liability", the registered keeper is presumed to be the owner of the vehicle for the purposes of enforcement. This presumption may be rebutted by the registered keeper.

Restricted Street

A street, or part of a street, in which parking is controlled for

- all of the time, marked by a double yellow line (DYL); or
- part of the time, marked by a single yellow line

The times of restriction are normally shown on yellow plates adjacent to the yellow line.

However,

- a plate is not now required for a DYL; and
- plates are not required in a Controlled Parking Zone where the times of restriction are the same as shown on the zone entry plates

Review

Either party to an appeal can apply for a review of an Adjudicator's decision. However, the grounds on which such an application may be made are limited. The application must be made within fourteen days after the decision was sent to the parties.

Road Traffic Act 1991 (RTA 1991)

The Act of Parliament that decriminalised certain parking offences, making them civil contraventions, enforceable by local authorities where a SPA or PPA Order is in force.

Road Traffic Regulation Act 1984 (RTRA 1984)

The Act of Parliament which provided many of the powers for councils to control parking in their area, which have now been incorporated in the decriminalised regime brought in by the Road Traffic Act 1991.

Special Parking Area (SPA)

An area approved by the Secretary of State for Transport within which the enforcement of most parking controls has been decriminalised and where enforcement may therefore be undertaken by the local authority.

Statement of liability

Part of the agreement signed by the hirer of a vehicle accepting liability for Penalty Charge Notices issued to the vehicle during the hire period. See 'Hire agreement' above.

Statutory Declaration

A declaration in response to an Order for Recovery made on one of the specified grounds. A valid statutory declaration cancels the Order for Recovery, the Charge Certificate and sometimes the Notice to Owner in parking contraventions and the Enforcement Notice in bus lane contraventions. It does not cancel the Penalty Charge Notice. It is a criminal offence to knowingly and wilfully make a false statutory declaration.

Traffic Enforcement Centre (TEC)

Situated currently at the County Court in Northampton, this is the centre where unpaid penalty charges are registered as debts at the County Court. This is an automated process, not requiring, or allowing an appearance by any party.

Traffic Management Order (TMO)

An order made by a local authority under the Road Traffic Regulation Act 1984 and which details the nature and extent of traffic and parking controls within the council's area. It is a contravention of these controls that may give rise to the issuing of a Penalty Charge Notice. The same orders are known as Traffic Regulation Orders (TROs) outside London.

TRACE

The centralised inquiry line run by the ALG in respect of vehicles removed by London boroughs under the RTA 1991.

Vehicle Registration Mark (VRM)

the number plate of a vehicle

Vehicle Excise Licence (VEL)

the tax disc of a vehicle which bears a unique serial number

Waiver

A temporary consent, granted by the council, to relax parking controls for a specified vehicle or motorist.

Warrant of Execution

Authority issued by the county court to enforce an unpaid debt, following registration at the TEC. Warrants must be in the possession of a certificated bailiff when attempts are made to recover the debt.

FOUR

POWERS OF THE POLICE & TRAFFIC WARDENS

The police have a number of powers aimed at keeping drivers and pedestrians safe on our roads. Here is an overview of situations where you may be pulled over by the police, plus advice on your rights and responsibilities. The police and traffic wardens enforce road traffic regulations. Traffic wardens are concerned mainly with stationary traffic offences and with assisting in traffic control and direction. The police deal with most moving vehicle offences.

In general, when dealing with these offences you have some options to those we have discussed with relation to speeding and parking. Make as many notes as you are able as to the identity of the officer involved using their collar number, time and date of where you were stopped. Photographic evidence, diagrams and witness statements are all in valuable should you wish to challenge the offence for which you have been reported.

The police have the power to stop anyone at any time – they don't need to give you a reason – and failing to stop is a criminal offence.

When pulled over by the police, you may be asked to produce documents including:-

- driving licence
- insurance certificate
- vehicle registration document

If you do not have these with you, you will be given seven days to produce them at a police station. If you feel you have been stopped too many times, you can make a complaint

Irrespective of rank the law considers all policemen to be "constables". The police have wide powers to control road traffic and can in general direct drivers to follow particular directions, prevent them from following certain routes, can stop them, request the removal of parked vehicles, and request the production of driving licenses and other documents and so on.

Failure to comply with any of these requirements is an offence which could lead to prosecution on a variety of charges including obstructing the police in their duties:

- A police constable in uniform can stop a moving vehicle on a road.

- Where a vehicle has been left on a road causing an obstruction or danger or is in contravention of a parking restriction or has broken down, the police can ask the driver or owner to remove the vehicle. If it appears to have been abandoned the police themselves may remove it or may arrange for it to be removed. (The local authority is also empowered to remove vehicles that appear to be abandoned.)

- The police can require the driver of a vehicle on a road to produce his driving licence and/or to state his date of birth if he fails to provide the licence at the time.

- They can request an "L" driver of a vehicle or the person accompanying him to produce his licence.

- They can request a person believed to have been the driver in an accident, or when a traffic offence was committed, to produce his driving licence. In both of these cases the licence may be produced immediately or within seven days at a police station nominated by him.

- They can request a driver to perform the driving test eyesight requirement if they suspect that his vision is deficient.

- Police constables in uniform can arrest any person driving or attempting to drive a motor vehicle on a road who is suspected of being a disqualified driver.

- They can arrest a person who takes a breathalyser test indicating that he has an excess of alcohol in the blood, and can also arrest a person who refuses to take a breath test.

- They can arrest a person driving or attempting to drive a motor vehicle on a road, or other public place if he is unfit to drive through the effects of drink or drugs.

- They can arrest a driver of a motor vehicle who commits an offence of dangerous, careless or inconsiderate driving if he will not give his name and address or provide his driving licence for examination.

Traffic wardens, appointed by the police authority, have powers to enforce the law in respect of:-

- vehicles parking without lights and reflectors

- vehicles obstructing a road

- vehicles waiting

- vehicles parked

- vehicles loading or unloading on a road or contravening the Vehicles (Excise) Act

- vehicles parked without paying meter charges

They may fulfil duties at street parking places and car pounds, act as school crossing patrols, and have the power to direct and regulate traffic. They can be empowered to make enquiries about a driver's identity and, when on duty at a car pound only, can demand to see driving licences. They can request a driver to give his name and address if he is believed to have committed an offence and can request the name and address of a pedestrian who ignores a traffic direction.

Traffic wardens may also issue fixed penalty tickets for the following non-endorsable driving offences:-

- leaving a vehicle parked at night without lights or reflectors
- waiting, loading or parking in prohibited areas
- unauthorised parking in controlled parking zone areas
- contravention of the Vehicles (Excise) Act 1971 by not displaying a current licence disc
- making U-turns in unauthorised places
- lighting offences with moving vehicles
- driving the wrong way in a one-way street
- over-staying on parking meters or feeding meters to obtain longer parking time than that permitted in the meter zone

When a fixed-penalty offence has been committed the vehicle owner is assumed to be the driver, unless the actual driver was given the ticket at the time of the offence. Vehicle owners must give information to the police on request about details of the driver of a vehicle at the time an offence was committed. The vehicle owner is liable to pay any penalty imposed if the driver fails to do so within twenty eight days. In the case of hired vehicles the hirer becomes the owner for these purposes. Alternatively, a statutory statement of ownership may be given (within twenty eight days) certifying that at the time of the alleged offence the vehicle was owned by somebody else (in which case the name of the previous or subsequent owner must be given) or, that the vehicle was at the time being used without the owner's knowledge or permission.

The police have the power to seize a vehicle if it is being used in an anti-social manner (causing alarm, harassment or distress). This includes inconsiderate driving and unauthorised off-road driving of cars, motorbikes etc.

Police can seize vehicles if drivers do not have an appropriate licence or insurance.

Police can 'breathalyse' you (ask you for a breath test) if they suspect you have been drinking if, for example, your driving seems erratic. You will be asked to give two valid samples of breath, and the lower result is the one on which any prosecution will be based.

If you fail the breath test, the police will take you to the police station where you will be charged and the evidence (the breath test) will be stored. You must leave your car until you are sober enough to move it, or another 'legal' driver can move it with your permission.

If you have twelve points on your licence within a three year period as a result of endorsable offences, your licence will usually be revoked for at least six months. Drink driving offences will result in mandatory disqualification from driving.

Serious road offences may result in imprisonment – such as causing death by dangerous driving. If your vehicle is defective, for example one of its indicators is broken, you may be issued with a vehicle defect rectification notice. This means you have to fix the fault and provide proof, such as a receipt from a mechanic saying the fault has been fixed, at a police station.

Forgery

A forgery is a written imitation passed off as though it was made by another person and was genuine. It is an offence to deceive intentionally by means of forgery, alteration or misuse any document or licence, vehicle test, plating or manufacturer's certificate, maintenance record, driving license, certificate of insurance or security. Such documents are invalid. It is also an offence to have in your possession (with intent to deceive) a forged or false document even if you did not personally perpetrate same.

False Statements

A false statement is one known to be untrue – a lie – and intended to deceive. It is an offence to make false statements knowingly for the purpose of obtaining or preventing the grant of any licence, to produce false evidence or to make false statements knowingly or to make a false entry in any record, or to withhold any material information for the purpose of obtaining a certificate of insurance (Road Traffic Act 1988). Any document, record, licence or certificate so obtained is invalid.

Useful terms

Here is a list of terms related to law enforcement for the professional driver. Know who and what you are dealing with!

ACPO

The Association of Chief Police Officers. This body is a "steering committee" of senior police officers that produces guidelines on how each constabulary should operate. However, ultimately it is down to the individual Chief Constable of each constabulary to set his own procedures, and that is why there is substantial regional variation in police procedures across the U.K.

Calibrated Speedometer

Police patrol cars are fitted with very accurate speedometers and it is perfectly acceptable for the police to use them to measure your speed. Please note that they must be following you and maintaining a constant distance.

Caution

The following words are referred to as the "caution":-

> *"You do not have to say anything but it may harm your defence if you do not mention now something you later rely on in court. Anything you do say may be given in evidence."*

CPS

The Crown Prosecution Service. This is the body that is supposedly "independent" of the police which prosecutes you on their behalf. We have no evidence that they are independent.

Disclosure

Under the law any evidence that the CPS is going to use to prosecute you must be made available to the defence prior to the trial so that they can prepare. The police collect evidence on behalf of the CPS, but that evidence becomes the property of the Crown when you are to be prosecuted. As a taxpayer you are entitled to a copy of the evidence (traffic video), so you can request a copy even if you have already been convicted.

All evidence is supposed to be kept for seven years after conviction, but that is probably also down to individual constabularies' procedures when it comes to Summary Offences.

Do not worry, we can tell just from the officer's statement if the time and distance device was being used. Do you remember more than one speed being quoted during a "follow check", or the words "by using my patrol car speedometer" appearing in the officer's statement?

Follow Check

This is exactly what it says. It is when the patrol car is following you and measuring your speed. Some constabularies instruct their officers to conduct a one mile follow check, but under the law that is not strictly necessary.

Again, get them to explain their procedures to you.

FPN

The Fixed Penalty Ticket (FPN)is a conditional offer made by the police. It is the minimum punishment for a speeding offence and attracts three penalty points and a £60 fine. If you have received a ticket from a speed camera you need to check it very carefully because the FPN can be issued up to six months after the alleged offence, unlike a standard NIP which must be issued within fourteen days.

Magistrates' Courts

The Magistrates' Court is the most junior of all courts - and the one that provides the most local service. All criminal cases begin before magistrates (magistrates were first appointed by the Justice of the Peace Act, 1361).

All speeding offences are handled by Magistrates' Courts.

NIP

Notice of Intended Prosecution. This means they are going to prosecute you for the offence. It can take two forms:-

- A written NIP (e.g. if you get a ticket from a speed camera)
- Verbal

Most constabularies send them out within fourteen days of the alleged offence - even if you were spoken to at the time by a police officer (see verbal NIP). They are usually sent by Recorded Delivery.

PACE

The Police and Criminal Evidence Act. This outlines the way police officers must behave when dealing with citizens and has caused the most confusion amongst police officers. For example, many have said "you must have been cautioned" as the caution is mandatory under PACE. But PACE may not apply to "Summary Offences" - speeding is one example of a summary offence.

Police Procedures

These are very important, and cause most of the confusion because different constabularies' procedures can be totally different. The legal minimum relating to speeding does not require many of the things outlined in individual constabularies' procedures. This is why it is very important that you ensure that the officer who stops you clearly explains his constabulary's procedures to you.

Skeleton Argument

This document outlines the defence's case in words that legal people like to use, and forces the prosecution to respond with its case.

Speeding

You are guilty of speeding once you travel at one mph over the posted speed limit, and for that reason the police refer to it as an "absolute offence". If a police officer tells you that they will not pull you over on a motorway at under 85 mph that is either their personal opinion or the policy of their constabulary. This is why they do not need any changes in legislation to introduce "zero tolerance".

Statement of Facts

Under the 1980 Magistrates Court Act this is required to accompany a summons and summarises the alleged offence. However, it is perfectly acceptable for a police officer's statement to form the only "statement of facts".

Target Vehicle

This is how the police refer to the vehicle they are following. If they stop you it was your vehicle.

Time and Distance Device

This refers to the speed measurement equipment used in all patrol cars in the UK. They measure the time and the distance of the "target vehicle" between two points and work out an average speed. They are all manually operated by the police officers in the patrol car. There are no automatic systems, because radar is not allowed to be used in moving vehicles in the UK.

Two examples of time and distance devices are:-

- ProVida
- VASCAR (the most commonly used)

Traffic Video

Patrol cars in the UK are now fitted with video recording equipment which records what happened. It records lots of other data in addition to the basic video. They can use the video to very accurately calculate your speed.

Verbal NIP

This is the one you have to listen carefully for. Under the law it is the legal minimum that you have to receive before a summons. The words are not clear and may confuse you.

They will be something like:-

> *"You will be reported for consideration of the question of prosecuting you for this offence."*

Although there appears to be need for "consideration" and a "question" to answer you may never hear anything else from the constabulary before you receive a court summons. Make sure that if you have anything to say for yourself, you say it after the verbal NIP. If a verbal warning is given at the time, it must be shown that the defendant understood it (Gibson v Dalton [1980]). Proof that they understood the charge will lie with the prosecution.

Viewing the Evidence

This section of the ACPO guidelines suggests that there is no actual legal right to view the evidence when you are stopped. However, make sure that you take the time to study the evidence. Explain that you may need a copy of the traffic video for independent verification of your speed. Even if they do not like that it is not up to them, as the evidence becomes the property of the Crown when you are prosecuted.

DRIVER'S PROTECTION MANUAL

FIVE

WHAT TO DO WHEN YOU ARE IN COURT

Unless the offence is very serious, carrying a possible prison term of two years or more, virtually all motoring offences that do go to court will be tried in the magistrates' court. Magistrates'courts deal with criminal, motoring and some civil cases. Cases are dealt with either by Justices of the Peace, who are unqualified and who are paid only expenses, or by District Judges (magistrates' courts) who receive some payment. In Northern Ireland, cases are heard by paid magistrates only. Magistrates' courts usually only deal with cases which arise in their own area. In Northern Ireland, in exceptional cases, they can deal with offences that occur in a number of areas, for example, where several burglaries have been committed across a number of areas.

The Crown Prosecution Service (CPS) is the government department that advises the police on possible prosecutions for criminal offences.

Created by the Prosecution of Offences Act 1985, the CPS reviews cases started by the police to ensure that the right defendants are prosecuted on the right charges and then prepares the cases for court.

If you are charged with a less serious offence, which would normally just be heard in a magistrates' court, you should know within six months whether you are to be prosecuted.

Typical offences tried by magistrates would be:-

- Drink Driving – driving whilst under the influence of alcohol.

- Speeding - not following the speed limits.

- Smoking and Driving - new laws have made it illegal to smoke for example if you use a company car or a taxi. Private vehicles are not yet affected.

- Tyres - illegal or defective tyres.

- Hand Held Mobile Phones - you must now use a hands free device to comply with the law.

- Driving under the influence of drugs.

If charged, you will get a written summons from the court. This will be posted to you or handed to you personally. The summons tells you what offences you have been charged with and gives the day and time that you have to be at court and the address of the court building.

It is advisable to get to court half an hour before the time you have been given. When you arrive, tell the usher that you are there. Usually they wear a black gown and have a clipboard telling them who they should expect. If you do not have a solicitor, ask to see the 'Duty Solicitor'. You may qualify for free legal advice, although this is not likely in most minor motoring offences.

When you attend court, you should dress smartly. Keep your hands by your side, not in your pockets and do not chew gum. When you are speaking to the magistrates, address them as 'Sir' or 'Madam'.

In the event that all of your efforts to get rid of the traffic ticket, the fixed penalty notice or other than document you have received through the post advising you that you have infringed traffic regulations, come to nothing, you are only left with two alternatives. One of these is to pay the fine and just move on, the second is to go to court to defend your case and at best win the case, if all else fails you would at least have the opportunity of being heard in mitigation with the possibility of a lesser fine, lesser period of disqualification or no disqualification at all. We have discussed the various decisions you have to make in this respect in previous chapters. Clearly there are some cases where the amount of the fine is possibly less than the cost of taking the matter to court will be, when you add up losing one or more days work and possibly employing a solicitor. Equally, as a professional driver, if the case carries a possible endorsement on your driving licence then clearly you have to do your utmost to either have the case overturned or two try and persuade the court not to add points to your licence and possibly disqualify you if this is an option.

You cannot disregard the court summons or fixed penalty notice. These will inevitably bring the full weight of the law upon your head and will almost certainly result in a heavier fine when the case does finally come to court, which it most certainly will sooner or later. As well as a heavier fine, you also run the risk of making yourself liable to arrest by the police. It would be less than impressive if you were in your place of work when the police came to arrest you and drag you off in handcuffs. So when the fixed penalty notice, the notice or court summons does arrive, begin planning how you will deal with it. In the case of a fixed penalty notice, one option available to you, apart of course from just paying the fine, is to admit the offence but not accept the amount of the fine. Let us say before we go any further that this is not a good option. It is highly unlikely that any court in the land will accept a reduction in what is after all a mandatory financial penalty laid down by the law. The chances are that you will be wasting your time and possibly incurring more expense as well.

If you decide to go to court on the basis that you do not feel that you committed the offence, or you feel that the prosecution case is not as strong as it could be and you have a good chance of beating it, you will then need to notify the court that you will be attending and put in a plea of not guilty. Whilst the next stage in the process is that you attend court, there is always the outside possibility, by no means unknown, that the Crown Prosecution Service may feel that the case is not as strong as it could be, especially in view of the fact that you yourself feel this to be the case, and it could be dropped. If this does not happen, you will then be appearing in front of the magistrates in due course.

As we have discussed in previous chapters, the key word here is preparation. You need to take every step to prepare every single tiny piece of evidence that may aid in your case. You need photographs, witness statements, drawings and plans of where the offence allegedly occurred. Now consider how you will present your case. Firstly, you should have used the time while you are waiting for the case to come to court to amass all of the evidence, photos and witness statements together with all relevant police reports that we have mentioned earlier. You are in court dressed in smart clothes and presenting a respectful attitude to the magistrates and court staff. You should remember that the magistrates and their staff are theoretically neutral, neither on your side or that of the police and Crown Prosecution Service. Whilst there will inevitably be some bias one way or the other, this is only human nature, you must go with this expectation in mind.

The other expectation you should have is that the police and Crown Prosecution Service emphatically are not neutral. They are bringing a case to prosecute and punish you, and will most certainly be doing their best to achieve this result. It would be unwise to expect any fairness or impartiality from the police, or indeed any kind of competence and efficiency. In fact, these aspects work in a contrary way stop lack of fairness and impartiality on the part of the police is something that you are in court to fight and defend yourself against. Lack of competence and efficiency on the part of the police or the Crown Prosecution Service is something that if you are able to detect it and offer evidence of this fact to the court could work very well in your favour. In many cases this has resulted in the case of being thrown out of court. Examples of this are when the police or CPS failed to issue the documents in the required time or issued documents that are flawed, for example the names and addresses or dates and times on them are incorrect.

Let us assume that you have pleaded not guilty, in the vast majority of cases there is little point in appearing in court without at least making this attempt to overturn the case against you. Your case will be heard by two or three magistrates. These are laypeople, not trained solicitors or judges, but are members of the public of good standing who have volunteered their services. They have received some training and are fully advised in the court by the clerk of the court who is a qualified solicitor. Some cases may be heard by a district judge who is paid.

In the court, the magistrates will sit at one end of the court facing you, with the clerk in front of them. The legal teams for the prosecution and defence will sit at tables in front of the clerk of the court and the witness stand will be to one side of the court. The other side is the dock. In practice, the charge against you will be read out with a summary of the details and you will be asked to plead guilty or not guilty. If you do plead not guilty you will be asked to present witnesses. You will also have a chance to cross examine the witnesses against you, which will of course include the police officers who first reported the offence.

If your offence is of a very serious nature it will be heard in a Crown Court. The main difference here is that Crown Court cases are generally more serious cases that can result in a lengthy term of imprisonment, and most importantly the verdict will be arrived at by a jury of twelve members of the public. You should note however that the majority of motoring offences cannot be tried in a Crown Court by jury. There are several important points to be borne in mind if you should find yourself in a Crown Court with the option of a Crown Court trial or appeal.

Firstly there is the question of expense. Unless you are defending yourself, you will need to hire a barrister as well as a solicitor to represent you. Whilst you could technically represent yourself in a Crown Court, the reality is that a case that has reached this far is likely to have serious consequences if it goes against you and you would be better by far been looking for a team that was experienced in your type of motoring offence. You should note that there are thousands of solicitors and barristers in the UK, but there are only a few that are highly experienced with very successful track records of winning motoring cases. Part of your preparation to your court appearance should be in research to find these kinds of people and making sure that you work with them to produce the most favourable result on the day. If you are able to find any kind of legal precedent that you feel makes the case against you invalid, you should present this as soon as practically possible. Although if you do have a good professional legal team it would not be unreasonable to hope that they were aware of legal precedents and would use them where necessary. However, take nothing for granted, research, research, research. Go over every single document that you have available to you.

Check and if necessary print copies of all of your photographs. Make sure that your plans of the scene of the offence are clear and professional. Make sure your witness statements are meticulously accurate and prepared in the correct format. It would be reasonable to assume that if you had a legal team that they had made all these checks themselves, but take nothing for granted. It is your career as a professional driver that is on the line as well as your bank balance. If you can manage to overturn the case and be found not guilty the CPS will of course have to pay your costs.

If necessary you can call the officer who reported you to court as a witness. In this case be absolutely certain you are calm, courteous and professional, showing respect for his position as a police officer. Your mission is to throw doubt on the accuracy of the police officer's statements. To this end you can question him or her about such things as his notebook, asking if it is an accurate comparison with the case they have presented to the court. You could ask questions about what you were wearing or the description of your vehicle and load when they reported the offence. Ask about their knowledge of the law as it applied under the conditions in which you were reported. Ask about the checks they made, if relevant, on their vehicle speedometers or speed check equipment both before and after they used it on that particular day. Compare their answers with the documentation you already have in this respect to see if there is any discrepancy. Provided the cross examination is conducted in a calm and courteous manner, you should be able to get away with asking many detailed questions.

As a defendant you do have the option of making a statement to the court, not under oath, about the circumstances of the alleged offence. This is a powerful option, as you cannot be cross examined on the facts as you give them. The negative side of his option is that it carries less weight than presenting your evidence in the witness box under oath, where you can be cross examined. However, despite the statement being given less weight than evidence given under oath it will be given strong consideration by the court and is a worthwhile option to consider, especially if you feel that a cross-examination could be tricky in your case. Either option carries a degree of risk and it is for you to consider the particular circumstances of the offence, the evidence against you and how you feel you can conduct yourself under the pressure of cross examination by a solicitor or barrister. Weigh up all of the odds, make the decision and then go with what you have decided without losing any sleep over it. Either option has its drawbacks and you cannot choose both.

In the unfortunate event that you are found guilty you will have the opportunity to make a statement in mitigation of the offence. When making this statement, be careful not to contradict any of the evidence you gave either under oath or in your statement to the court. This is unlikely to help when the magistrates pass sentence.

SIX

THE DRIVER AND THE LAW

In this chapter we will look at the various motoring laws as they apply to private motorists. Clearly, if you are to avoid falling foul of the law you need to be clear of exactly what the law is. Ignorance of the law is no defence and if you are fully aware of exactly what you are up against you are more likely to be able to take steps to avoid breaking the law. Or at least, to be careful.

Driver Licencing

A licence showing a full or provisional driving entitlement must be held by any person wishing to drive a motor vehicle on public roads in the UK or within Europe. Drivers of good vehicles require a current licence showing an LGV (large goods vehicle) vocational driving entitlement (either full or provisional). Any person found to be driving without a licence or without one covering the correct category of vehicle faces heavy penalties.

The employer of any person required to drive for business purposes must ensure that his employees, irrespective of their function, status or seniority, are correctly licenced. The fact that a driver may be disqualified, or has allowed his licence to lapse, is no defence for the employer against prosecution for allowing an unlicenced person to drive.

Offences

Driving or causing or permitting another person to drive a vehicle without a current and valid driving licence is an offence.

Invalidation of Insurance

Driving without a current and valid driving licence covering the category of vehicle driven can invalidate insurance cover (which is itself an offence and is usually added to the charges) and could result in rejection of any accident or damage claim by the insurance company.

Legislative Changes Since 1990

Since 1st April 1991 the pink and green European "unified" driving licence (Euro-licence), which shows all entitlements to drive has been issued from the DVLA, Swansea. Traffic Commissioners (TCs) no longer issue large goods and passenger vehicle licences. The Euro-licence carries the words "European Communities Model" and has "driving licence" printed in the language of the country of issue, that of all EU nations, Greek and Gaelic on the front. British-issued Euro-licences also show, where appropriate, provisional driving entitlements and any endorsements of penalty points or licence disqualification made by the courts. This part of the document is called the "counterpart" and is green.

Existing UK Licence Holders

For a large proportion of British ordinary driving licence holders who currently hold "licences-for-life", the changes mentioned above will not be noticed unless or until they apply to change the details on their licence. At that time they will be issued the Euro-licence.

The licencing provisions described in this section are principally contained in the:-

- Road Traffic Act 1988
- Road Traffic (Driver Licencing and Information Systems) Act 1989
- Road Traffic (New Drivers) Act 1995
- Motor Vehicles (Driving licences) Regulations 1996 as amended
- Motor Vehicles (Driving licences) (Large Goods and Passenger

Carrying Vehicles) Regulations 1990 (which deal with entitlements to drive large goods vehicles over 7.5 tons gross weight and passenger carrying vehicles used for hire and reward operations) plus a number of subsequent amendments

Changes to the licence system made by this legislation involved significant alteration in vocational (HGV/PSV) licencing. The terminology changed so that heavy goods vehicles (HGV) and public service vehicles (PSV) are now called large goods vehicles (LGV) and passenger carrying vehicles (PCV). Additionally, goods vehicles are no longer classified by the number of axles.

Definitions

For driver licencing purposes:-

- a "large goods vehicle" is "a motor vehicle (not being a medium-sized goods vehicle)which is constructed or adapted to carry or haul goods and the permissible maximum weight of which exceeds 7.5 tons"

- a medium-sized goods vehicle is defined as one having a permissible maximum weight exceeding 3.5 tons but not exceeding 7.5 tons.

- a large passenger carrying vehicle has been constructed or adapted to carry more than 16 passengers;

- a small passenger carrying vehicle carries passengers for hire or reward and has been constructed or adapted to carry more than 8 but not more than 16 passengers

Photographs on Licences

To help eliminate misuse and fraud the new British-issued driving licences carry the holder's photograph. (Licences in Northern Ireland already carry a photograph.) Plastic photocard driving licences for British holders were launched on 23rd July 1998. These will eventually

replace the current licence, although existing paper licences will remain valid until they expire or are revoked.

Standard licence information includes the individual's name, address and date of birth, the vehicles they are entitled to drive, and the date of issue and expiration. All this is against a pink background in one of the EU's official languages (plus one other language if required). The nationality symbol for the country of issue is shown ("UK" will be used rather than "GB" as shown on vehicle nationality plates) on a blue background and surrounded by the EU's 12 gold stars, together with the holder's photograph.

The new-type licence will be issued to new licence applicants and to existing licence holders who apply for replacements or who wish to change the details on their licence - existing licences will not be recalled for change.

The Issuing Authority

The Driver and Vehicle Licencing Agency (the DETR's Executive Agency - DVLA), Swansea issues vocational driving entitlements. The TCs still retain a disciplinary role in regard to such entitlements.

Age Limits for Drivers

Certain minimum ages are specified by law for drivers of various categories of motor vehicle:

Invalid carriage or moped*	16 years
Motor cycle other than a moped* (over 50cc engine capacity)	17 years
Small passenger vehicle or small goods vehicle (not exceeding 3.5 tons gross weight and not adapted to carry more than nine people including the driver)	17 years
Agricultural tractor	17 years

Medium-size goods vehicle (exceeding 3.5 tons but not exceeding 7.5 tons gross weight)	18 years
Other goods vehicles (over 7.5 tons gross weight) and passenger vehicles with more than nine passenger seats	21 years

*The definition of moped is: in the case of a vehicle first registered before 1st August 1977, a motorcycle with an engine cylinder capacity not exceeding 50cc equipped with pedals by means of which it can be propelled. In the case of a vehicle first registered on or after 1st August 1977, a motorcycle which does not exceed the following limits: kerbside weight 250kg; cylinder capacity (if applicable) 50cc.

If a goods vehicle and trailer combination exceeds 3.5 tons permissible maximum weight the driver must be 18 years of age; if such a combination exceeds 7.5 tons the driver must be 21 years of age (and will also need to hold an LGV driving entitlement).

Members of the armed forces are exempt from the 21 years age limit for driving heavy goods vehicles when such driving is in aid of the civil community. The limit is then reduced to 17 years. Similarly, exemption from the 21-year minimum age limit applies to learner LGV drivers of vehicles over 7.5 tons gross weight if they are undergoing registered training by their employer or by a registered training establishment. In this case the minimum age is 18 years.

Vehicle Categories/Groups for Driver Licencing
For driver licencing purposes vehicles are defined according to specified categories shown on licences by capital letters.

Motorcycles
A   Motorcycles (with or without sidecar) and scooters but excluding vehicles in category K. Additional categories covered: B1, K, P

A1   Light motorcycles not over 125cc and 11kW (14.6bhp). Additional category covered: P

Cars and Light Vans

B   Motor vehicles up to 3.5 tons mass and with not more than eight seats (excluding the driver's seat) including drawing a trailer of up to 750kg mass. Including combinations of category B vehicles and a trailer where the combined weight does not exceed 3.5 tons and the weight of the trailer does not exceed the unladen weight of the towing vehicle. Additional categories covered: F, K, P

B1   Motor tricycles and three/four-wheeled cars and vans up to 550kg unladen with a design speed not exceeding 50kph and, if fitted with an internal combustion engine, a cubic capacity not exceeding 50cc. Additional categories covered: K, P

B+E   Motor vehicles in category B drawing a trailer over 750kg where the combination does not come within category B.

Medium Goods Vehicles

C1   Medium goods vehicles between 3.5 tons and 7.5 tons (including drawing trailer of up to 750kg - maximum weight of the combination must not exceed 8.25 tons).

C 1 +E   Medium goods vehicles between 3.5 tons and 7.5 tons and drawing a trailer over 750kg but which does not exceed the unladen weight of the towing vehicle - maximum weight of the combination must not exceed 12 tons. Additional category covered: B+E

Large Goods Vehicles

C   Large goods vehicles over 3.5 tons (but excluding vehicles in categories D, F, G and H) including those drawing a trailer of up to 750kg.

C+E Large goods vehicles in category C drawing a trailer exceeding 750kg. Some C+E licences, where the holder was previously qualified to drive vehicles in old HGV class 2 or 3, show a restriction limiting driving to drawbar combinations only. Additional category covered: B + E

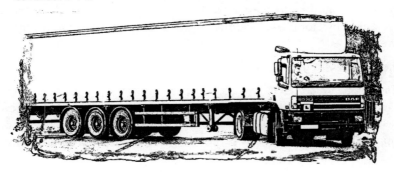

Minibuses

D1   Passenger vehicles with between 9 and 16 seats including drawing trailer up to 750kg.

D1+EMotor vehicles in category D1 drawing a trailer over 750kg - the weight of the trailer must not exceed the unladen weight of the towing vehicle and the maximum weight of the combination must not exceed 12 tons. Additional category covered: B+E

Passenger Vehicles

D   Passenger vehicles with more than eight seats including drawing a trailer up to 750kg.

D+E Passenger vehicles in category D drawing a trailer over 750kg. Additional category covered: B+E

Other Vehicles

F   Agricultural or forestry tractors but excluding any vehicle in category H.

G   Road rollers.

H   Track-laying vehicles steered by their tracks.

K   Mowing machine or pedestrian-controlled vehicle (with up to three wheels and not over 410kg).

L   Electrically propelled vehicles.

P   Mopeds.

Vehicle/trailer weights, unless otherwise specified, are to be taken as the maximum authorized mass (mam) which is the permissible maximum weight (pmw) for the vehicle/trailer - commonly referred to as the "gross weight."

Restricted Categories for Post-1997 Drivers

Since 1st January 1997, drivers who pass the car and light vehicle test (vehicles up to 3.5 tons pmw) may not drive heavier vehicles without securing additional driving categories on their licence. This restriction applies only to those who pass the test after the specified date and does no apply retrospectively.

Drivers who pass their car test (category B) may not drive minibuses (D1), medium-sized goods vehicles (C1), or tow large (over 750kg) trailers (B+E, C +E and D1+E). without testing for those categories.

Any driver wishing to drive a vehicle towing a heavy trailer (gross weight over 750kg) must first pass a test in the associated rigid vehicle. Learner drivers in categories B, C1, C, D1 and D cannot drive a vehicle towing a trailer of any size.

Towed and Pushed vehicles

A person who steers a vehicle being towed (whether it has broken down or even has vital parts missing) is "driving" for licencing purposes and therefore needs to hold current and valid driving entitlement covering that category of vehicle. Conversely, a person pushing a vehicle from the out side (with both feet on the ground) is not "driving" or "using" the vehicle.

Learner Drivers

Learner drivers must hold a provision: green "counterpart" of the licence.

Full category C LGV entitlement h place of a provisional entitlement for l C+E (drawbar combinations and arti in categories B and C1 cannot be us learning to drive vehicles in categori entitlement for these classes is requir

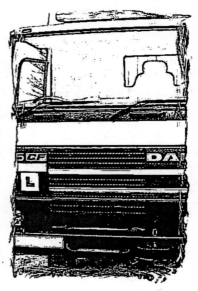

When driving on public roads learn the holder of a full entitlement cove and must not drive a vehicle drawi articulated vehicles or agricultural tra

An approved "L" plate must be displa driven by a learner driver. Learners display a "D" plate.

Learner drivers (of category B and C1 vehicles) are not allowed to drive on motorways. However, learner LGV drivers seeking a licence for category C and C+E vehicles and who hold full entitlements in licence categories B and C1, may drive such vehicles on motorways while under instruction.

Compulsory Re-tests for Offending New Drivers

Newly qualified drivers with six or more penalty points within two years of passing the test revert to learner status (with the display of "L" plates and the need to be accompanied by a qualified driver) and have to re-pass both the theory and the practical driving test.

Supervision of "L" Drivers

Qualified drivers supervising learner drivers in cars, and in light, medium and large goods vehicles, must be at least 21 years old with full driving entitlement for a continuous period of at least three years (excluding any periods of disqualification). Those accompanying learner LGV drivers must have held a relevant entitlement continuously since 6 April 1998.

Application for Licences and Vocational Entitlements

Applications for all driving licences have to be made to Swansea on Form D1 (obtainable from main post offices, direct from Swansea or from Local Vehicle Registration Offices).

Questions concern personal details of the applicant, the type of licence required, any previous licence held and whether the applicant is currently disqualified. LGV/PCV entitlement applicants are asked about any convictions recorded against them.

Health Declaration

Applicants are asked to declare information whether they have:-

- had an epileptic event
- sudden attacks of disabling giddiness, fainting or blackouts
- severe mental handicap
- had a pacemaker, defibrillator or anti-ventricular tachycardia device fitted
- diabetes controlled by insulin
- angina (heart pain) while driving
- a major or minor stroke
- Parkinson's disease
- any other chronic neurological condition
- a serious problem with memory
- serious episodes of confusion;
- any type of brain surgery, brain tumour or severe head injury involving hospital in-patient treatment
- any severe psychiatric illness or mental disorder
- continuing or permanent difficulty in the use of arms or legs which affects the ability to control a vehicle safely
- been dependent on or misused alcohol, illicit drugs or chemical substances in the previous three years (excluding drink/driving

offences)

- any visual disability which affects both eyes (short/long sight and colour blindness do not have to be declared)
- sight in only one eye
- any visual problems affecting either eye
- angina
- any heart condition or had a heart operation

Where a licence applicant has previously declared a medical condition they are required to state what the condition is, whether it has worsened, and whether any special controls have been fitted to the applicant's vehicle since the last licence was issued. By recommendation of the DVLA's Drivers Medical Branch following a heart attack or heart operation driving should not be undertaken for at least one month. Driving may be resumed afterwards if recovery has been uncomplicated and the patient's own doctor approves. A driver suffering from angina may continue to drive (whether he is receiving treatment or not) unless attacks occur while driving, in which case he must notify the DVLA immediately and stop driving. A driver who suffers sudden attacks of disabling giddiness, fainting, falling, loss of awareness or confusion must notify the DVLA immediately and stop driving. Any driver doubts his ability to drive safely is advised to discuss the matter with his own doctor who has access to medical advice from the DVLA.

Alcohol Problems

A person with repeated convictions for drink-driving offences may be required to satisfy the DVLA (with certification from his own doctor) that he does not have an "alcohol problem" before his licence is restored.

Other Medical Conditions

Other disabilities which may cause failure of the driver's medical examination include:-

- sudden attacks of vertigo
- heart disease which causes disabling weakness or pain
- a history of coronary thrombosis
- the use of hypertensive drugs for blood pressure treatment
- serious arrhythmia
- severe mental disorder
- severe behavioural problems
- alcohol dependency
- inability to refrain from drinking and driving
- drug abuse and dependency
- psychotropic medicines taken in quantities likely to impair fitness to drive safely

A licence will be refused to a driver liable to sudden attacks of disabling giddiness or fainting unless these can be controlled.

Those with a cardiac pacemaker are advised to discontinue LGV driving, although driving vehicles below the 7.5 tonne LGV threshold is permitted if the pacemaker controls disabling attacks and the driver's condition is subject to regular review by a cardiologist.

Notification of New or Worsening Medical Conditions

Once a licence of any type has been granted the holder is required to notify the Drivers Medical Group, DVLA at Swansea, of the onset, or worsening, of any medical condition likely to cause danger when driving. Failure to do so is an offence.

Examples include:-

- giddiness
- fainting

- blackouts
- epilepsy
- diabetes
- strokes
- multiple sclerosis
- Parkinson's disease
- heart disease
- angina
- coronaries
- high blood pressure
- arthritis
- disorders of vision
- mental illness
- alcoholism
- drug-taking
- the loss or loss of use of any limb

A doctor may advise a patient to report his condition to the DVLA or such a report may be made directly by the doctor. In either case the driving licence will have to be surrendered until the condition clears. There is no requirement to notify the DVLA of temporary illnesses or disabilities such as sprained or broken limbs where a full recovery is expected within three months. Enquiries about medical conditions can be raised with the Drivers Medical Group at the DVLA.

Medical Appeals and Information

The Drivers Medical Group of the DVLA makes the final decision on any medical matter concerning driving licences. Appeals may be made within six months in England and Wales to a magistrate's court, and within 21 days in Scotland to a sheriff's court. In other cases the driver may be given the opportunity to present further medical evidence for consideration.

Illegal Drugs

Among the illegal drugs which may be detected and which can adversely affect driving are:-

- Cannabis - produces slow reaction times.
- Cocaine - may increase reaction times, but severely affects accuracy and judgment. Potentially cause hallucinations.
- Amphetamines - may increase reaction times in the short term, but severely affects accuracy and judgment.
- Ecstasy - may increase reaction times, but severely affects accuracy and judgment.
- Heroin - produces reduced reaction times and causes drowsiness and sleep.

Prescribed Drugs

Prescribed tranquillizers, sedatives and anti-depressants, as well as diabetes and epilepsy drugs, may have an adverse effect on a driver's judgment and reactions. These include a number of anti-anxiolytic benzodiazepines (prescribed to reduce stress and anxiety) including Valium, Librium and Ativan.

The sedative effect of these drugs is substantially compounded by the addition of alcohol, even when taken in relatively small quantities, resulting in a potentially significant loss of coordination. Similarly, sleeping tablets (Diazepam, Temazepam and Nitrazepam) including the new drug Zopiclone may also have a continuing sedative effect on a driver the following morning.

A whole range of other proprietary medicines such as painkillers, antihistamines, cold and flu remedies, eye-drops, cough medicines and common painkillers taken in sufficient quantities may have similar effects.

If a driver feels drowsy, dizzy, confused, or suffers other side effects that could affect his reaction times or judgment, he should not drive.

Eyesight Requirement

The statutory eyesight requirement for ordinary licence holders is for the driver to be able to read, in good daylight (with glasses or contact lenses if worn), a standard motor vehicle number plate from 20.5 meters (67 feet). It is an offence to drive with impaired eyesight and the police can require a driver to take a roadside eyesight test. If glasses or contact lenses are needed they must be worn at all times while driving.

Eyesight Standards for Vocational Licence Holders

Tougher eyesight standards for LGV and PCV drivers were introduced from 1st January 1997. Specifically, drivers of vehicles in categories C, C1, C+E, C1+E, D, D1, D+E and D1+E (trucks over 3.5 tons and passenger vehicles with more than nine seats) must have eyesight which is at least:

- 6/9 on the Snellen scale in the better eye;* and
- 6/12 on the Snellen scale in the other eye;* and
- 3/60 in each eye without glasses or contact lenses

*These standards may be met with glasses or contact lenses if worn.

Individuals must be able to read the top line of an optician's chart with each eye from a distance of at least 3m without the aid of glasses or contact lenses. Wearers of spectacles or contact lenses must have vision of at least 6/9 in the better eye and at least 6/12 in the weaker eye (reading the sixth line of the chart at 6 meters.) All drivers must have a field of vision of at least 120° (horizontal) and 20° (vertical) in each eye with no double vision.0

Licence Validity

Full driving entitlements are valid from the date of issue until the applicant's 70th birthday. After 70 ordinary entitlement holders must make a new application and, if granted, each subsequent licence will be valid for three years.

Production of Driving Licences

Both the police and enforcement officers of the Vehicle Inspectorate (VI) can request a driver - and a person accompanying a provisional entitlement holder - to produce his licence showing his ordinary and vocational entitlements to drive. If he is unable to do so at the time, he may produce them without penalty if the request was by:-

- a police officer, at a police station of his choice within seven days
- an enforcement officer, at the Traffic Area Office within ten days

A police officer can ask a driver to state his or her date of birth. British ordinary driving licences carry a coded number which indicates the holder's surname and date of birth. The name and address of the vehicle owner can also be requested.

When required by a VI examiner to produce his licence, an LGV entitlement holder may be required to give his date of birth and to sign the examiner's record sheet to verify the fact of the licence examination. This should not be refused. Licence holders apprehended for endorsable fixed penalty (yellow ticket) offences are required to produce their driving licence to the police officer at that time or within seven days to a police station and to surrender the licence for which they will be given a receipt. Failure to do so means that the fixed penalty procedure will not be followed and a summons for the offence will be issued requiring a court appearance. Drivers summoned to appear in court for driving and road traffic offences must produce their driving licence to the court at least one day before the hearing.

Driving Licence Penalty Points and Disqualification

Driving licence holders may be penalised following conviction by a court for offences committed on the road with a motor vehicle. Penalties range from:-

- the issue of fixed penalty notices for non-endorsable offences (which do not require a court appearance unless the charge is contested and incur no driving licence penalty points although the relevant fixed penalty has to be paid)
- to those for endorsable offences when penalty points are added on the licence counterpart and the fixed penalty is incurred or a heavy fine imposed on conviction if a court appearance is made

In other cases, licence disqualification and in serious instances imprisonment, may follow conviction in a magistrates' court or indictment in a higher court. Holders of vocational driving entitlements may be separately penalised for relevant offences, which could result in such entitlements being suspended or revoked. In serious circumstances the holder may be disqualified from holding a vocational entitlement.

The Penalty Points System on Conviction and Disqualification

The Road Traffic Offenders Act 1988 (with further provisions relating to driving offences in the Road Traffic Act 1991) prescribes penalty points following conviction for motoring offences. The penalty points system grades road traffic offences according to their seriousness on a scale from two to ten points. Once a maximum of twelve penalty points has accumulated within a three-year period from the date of the first offence to the current offence, disqualification of the licence for at least six months is automatic.

Most offences rate a fixed number of penalty points to ensure consistency and to simplify the administration, but a discretionary range applies to a few offences where the gravity may vary from one case to another. Unless the court decides otherwise, when a driver is convicted of more than one offence at the same hearing, only the points relative to the most serious offence will normally be endorsed on the licence. Once a period of disqualification has been imposed, the driver starts fresh and those points will not be counted again.

To discourage repeated offences, however, the courts impose progressively longer disqualification periods in future instances of maximum accrued points. (Twelve months for subsequent disqualifications within three years; 24 months for a third disqualification within three years).

Licence Endorsement Codes and Penalty Points

Following conviction for an offence, the driver's licence green counterpart will be endorsed by the convicting court with a code and number of penalty points imposed.

Disqualification

The endorsing of penalty points will also arise on conviction for offences where disqualification is discretionary. In this case the offender's driving licence will be endorsed with four points. The courts are still free to disqualify immediately if the circumstances justify

Offences (Road Traffic Offenders Act 1988, Sch 2) carrying obligatory disqualification include:

- Causing death by dangerous driving and manslaughter.
- Dangerous driving within three years of a similar conviction.
- Driving or attempting to drive while unfit through drink or drugs.
- Driving or attempting to drive with more than the permitted breath- alcohol level.
- Failure to provide a breath, blood or urine specimen.
- Racing and speed trials on the highway.

Driving while disqualified is a serious offence that can result in a fine at level five on the standard scale, six months imprisonment, or both.

Special Reasons for Non-disqualification

The courts have discretion in exceptional mitigating circumstances not to impose a disqualification. The mitigating circumstance must not be one which attempts to make the offence appear less serious and no account will be taken of hardship other than exceptional hardship. Pleading that you have a wife and children to support or that you will lose your job is not generally considered to be exceptional hardship.

If account has previously been taken of circumstances in mitigation of a disqualification, the same circumstances cannot be considered again within three years.

Where a court decides, in exceptional circumstances, not to disqualify a convicted driver, four penalty points will be added to the driver's licence in lieu of the disqualification.

DRIVING OFFENCES

Dangerous Driving

Since 1st July 1992 "reckless driving" has been termed "dangerous" driving. Such a charge may be levied if the driving "falls far short of what would be expected of a competent and careful driver, and it would be obvious to a competent and careful driver that driving in that way would be dangerous" or "if it was obvious to a competent and careful driver that driving the vehicle in its current state would be dangerous."

"Dangerous" refers to danger either of injury to any person or of serious damage to property. The principal offences to which this relates are dangerous driving and causing death by dangerous driving.

Interfering with Vehicles

It is an offence for any person to cause danger to road users by way of intentionally and without lawful authority placing objects on a road, interfering with motor vehicles, or directly or indirectly interfering with traffic equipment such as road signs.

Penalties

Penalties are heavy. Causing death by careless driving while under the influence of drink or drugs carries a maximum penalty of up to five years in prison and/or a fine. For causing a danger to road users the maximum penalty is up to seven years imprisonment and/or a fine. In addition to disqualification and the endorsement of penalty points, courts may impose fines and, for certain offences, imprisonment. The maximum fine for most offences is determined by reference to a scale set out in the Criminal Justice Act 1991. Offences such as dangerous driving, failing to stop after an accident or failure to report an accident, and drink-driving offences, carry the maximum fine, as do certain vehicle construction, use offences (overloading, insecure loads, using a vehicle in a dangerous condition) and using a vehicle without insurance.

New Driver Penalties

The Road Traffic (New Drivers) Act 1995 concerns drivers who first passed their driving test on or after 1st June 1997. Where such drivers acquire six or more penalty points within two years of passing the test the DVLA will automatically revoke the licence on notification by a court or fixed penalty office. Such drivers have to surrender their full licence and obtain a provisional licence to start driving again as a learner. They will have to pass both the theory and practical tests again.

Penalty points counting towards the total of six include any incurred before passing the test, if this was not more than three years before the latest penalty point offence. Points imposed after the probationary period will also count if the offence was committed during that period.

Passing the retest will not remove the penalty points from the licence.

Short Period Disqualification (SPD)

If a driver is disqualified for less than fifty six days, the court will stamp the counterpart of his driving licence and return it to him. The stamp will show how long disqualification is to last. The licence does not have to be renewed when the SPD ends - it becomes valid again the day following expiration of the disqualification.

Removal of Penalty Points and Disqualifications

Penalty points can be removed after a specified waiting period - four years from the date of the offence, except in the case of reckless/dangerous driving convictions when the four years is taken from the date of conviction. Endorsements for alcohol-related offences must remain on a licence for eleven years. Licences returned after disqualification will show no penalty points but previous disqualifications (within four years) will remain and if a previous alcohol/drugs driving offence disqualification has been incurred, this will remain on the licence for eleven years.

Application may be made for reinstatement after varying periods depending on the duration of the disqualification as follows:-

- Less than two years - no prior application time.
- Less than four years - after two years have elapsed.
- Between four years and ten years - after half the time has

elapsed.

- In other cases - after five years have elapsed.

The courts are empowered to require a disqualified driver to retake the driving test, and following the introduction of provisions contained in the Road Traffic Act 1991, it is now mandatory for them to impose "extended" re-tests for the most serious offences, namely, dangerous driving, causing death by dangerous driving and manslaughter by the driver of a motor vehicle (in Scotland, the charge is culpable homicide).

Re-tests for Offending Drivers

Where drivers are convicted of the offences of manslaughter, causing death by dangerous driving or dangerous driving and mandatory disqualification is imposed, an "extended" re-test (involving at least one hour's driving) must be taken. This also applies to drivers disqualified by penalty points. Courts may order drivers disqualified for lesser offences to take an ordinary driving test.

Drink-Driving and Breath Tests

It is an offence to drive or to attempt to drive when the level of alcohol in the breath is more than 35 micrograms per 100 millilitres. This is determined by means of an initial breath test, conducted on the spot when the driver is stopped, and later substantiated by a breath-testing machine (Lion Intoximeter) at a police station. The breath/alcohol limit equates to the blood/alcohol limit of 80 milligrams of alcohol in 100 millilitres of blood or the urine/alcohol limit of 107 milligrams of alcohol in 100 millilitres of urine.

Failure to Produce a Breath Sample and Low Breath-Rest Readings

If the person suspected of an alcohol-related offence cannot, due to health reasons, produce a breath sample, or if a breath test shows a reading of not more than 50 micrograms of alcohol per 100 millilitres of breath, he is given the opportunity of an alternative test, either blood or urine, for laboratory analysis. This test can only be carried out at a police station or a hospital and the decision as to which alternative is chosen rests with the police (unless a doctor present determines a blood test cannot or should not be taken). Similarly, if a breath test of a driver shows the proportion of alcohol to be no more than 50 micrograms in 100 millilitres of breath, the driver can request an alternative test (blood or urine).

Prosecution for Drink-Driving Offences

Prosecution will follow test failure resulting in a fine or imprisonment and automatic disqualification from driving. Failure to submit to a breath test and to a blood or urine test are serious offences, and drivers will find themselves liable to heavy penalties on conviction and potentially long-term disqualification or driving licence endorsement (endorsements for such offences remain on a driving licence for eleven years).

The police do not have powers to carry out breath tests at random but they do have powers to enter premises to require a breath test from a person suspected of driving while impaired, or who has been driving or been in charge of a vehicle that has been involved in an accident in which another person has been injured.

Drink-Driving Disqualification

Conviction for a first drink-driving offence will result in a minimum one year period of disqualification; a second or subsequent offence longer periods of disqualification. If the previous conviction took place within ten years of the current offence the disqualification must be for at least three years.

Drivers convicted twice for drink-driving offences may have their driving licence revoked altogether. Offenders who are disqualified twice within a ten year period and those found to have an exceptionally high level of alcohol in the body (more than two and a half times over the limit), or those who twice refuse to provide a specimen, will be classified as high-risk offenders (HROs) by the Driver and Vehicle Licencing Agency. They will be required to show that they no longer have an "alcohol problem" by means of a medical examination (including blood analysis of liver enzymes) by a DVLA-approved doctor before licence restoration.

Penalties Against Vocational Entitlements

Where a licence holder is disqualified from driving following conviction for offences committed with cars or other light vehicles, or as a result of penalty points, any vocational entitlement held is automatically lost until the licence is reinstated. Additionally, the holder of an LGV/PCV vocational entitlement may have this revoked or suspended by the DVLA without reference to the TC and be disqualified from holding such entitlement, for a fixed or indefinite period, at any time, on the grounds of misconduct or physical disability. Furthermore, a person can be refused a new LGV/PCV driving entitlement following licence revocation, again either indefinitely or for some other period of time which the Secretary of State (via the DVLA) specifies. A new vocational test may be ordered before the entitlement is restored.

Disqualification from holding an LGV vocational entitlement does not prevent a licence holder from continuing to drive vehicles within the category B and C1 entitlements.

The TCs continue to play a disciplinary role in regard to driver conduct, but only at the request of the DVLA. They have powers to call drivers to a public inquiry (PI) to give information and to answer questions as to their conduct. Their duty is to report back to the DVLA if they consider that an LGV/PCV entitlement should be revoked or the holder disqualified from holding an entitlement - the DVLA must follow the TC's recommendation in these matters.

Failure to attend a PI when requested to do so (unless a reasonable excuse is given) means that the DVLA will automatically refuse a new vocational entitlement or suspend or revoke an existing one.

Large goods vehicle drivers who have been off the road for a period of time after being disqualified must prove themselves capable of driving small goods vehicles legally and safely for a period of time before their LGV driving entitlement may be restored by the TCs.

Rules on disciplining LGV entitlement holders require TCs to follow a set of recommended guidelines in imposing penalties. Under these rules, and where there are no aggravating circumstances, a driver being disqualified for twelve months or less should be sent a warning letter with no further disqualification of the LGV entitlement. Where a driving disqualification is for more than one year, the offender should be called to appear before the TC and he should incur an additional suspension, amounting to between one and three months. The intention is to allow the person to regain his driving skills and road sense in a car before driving a heavy vehicle again.

Where two or more driving disqualifications of more than eight weeks have been incurred within the past five years, and the combined total of disqualification exceeds twelve months, the driver should be called to a PI and a further period of LGV driving disqualification imposed amounting to between three and six months.

In the case of new LGV entitlements, for applicants with nine or more penalty points on their ordinary licence, the guidelines recommend the TC issue a warning as to future conduct or suggest that the applicant tries again when the penalty points total has been reduced.

Removal of LGV Driving Licence Disqualification

Drivers disqualified from holding an LGV/PCV entitlement may apply to have the disqualification removed after two years if it was for less than four years, or after half the period if the disqualification was for more than four years but less than ten. In any other case including disqualification for an indefinite period an application for its removal cannot be made for five years. If an application for the removal fails, another application cannot be made for three months. The DVLA will not necessarily readily restore LGV/PCV driving entitlements on application following disqualification. An applicant may be called to a PI by a TC who will inquire into the events which led to the disqualification and who may also decide that the applicant must wait longer before applying again, must spend a period driving small (up to 7.5 ton) vehicles, or must take a new LGV/PCV driving test to regain the vocational entitlement.

Appeals

If the DVLA refuses to grant an application for an LGV/PCV driving entitlement or revokes, suspends or limits an existing entitlement, the applicant or entitlement holder may appeal under the Road Traffic Act 1988. He must notify the DVLA and any TC involved of his intention to appeal. The appeal can then be made to a magistrates' court acting for the petty sessions in England or Wales, or in Scotland to the local sheriff.

Road traffic offences and legal action

When road traffic-related offences are committed alternative procedures may be followed by the police (or traffic wardens where appropriate) in the way of legal action. Depending on the nature of the offence, the offender may be issued with a fixed-penalty notice or reported for prosecution and required to answer directly to the court.

Fixed-penalty System

Fixed-penalty notices (tickets) may be issued for a large number of traffic, motoring and vehicle offences. Generally these will be issued by the police but traffic wardens are empowered to do so for some offences. When offences are committed, the driver is given a notice which specifies the offence, an indication whether it is a driving licence endorsable or non-endorsable offence (by the notice colour and wording), and the penalty which has to be paid. If the driver is not available the ticket may be attached to the vehicle windscreen, but the driver is still responsible for payment. Should the driver of a vehicle fail to pay, responsibility for payment rests with the registered vehicle keeper (the person/company whose name is on the registration document).

Fixed-penalty Procedure

The police (and to a certain extent, the traffic wardens) operate the fixed-penalty system for dealing with road traffic and related offences. Some two hundred and fifty motoring offences are included, divided into driving licence endorsable and non-endorsable offences. The former involves the police issuing a yellow penalty ticket for which a penalty is payable and the driving licence being confiscated and returned with the appropriate penalty points added when the penalty is paid.

If the offender does not have his driving licence with him a penalty notice will not be issued there but at the police station when the licence is produced within seven days. For non-endorsable offences a white ticket (involving a lesser penalty) is issued to the driver, if present, or is fixed to the vehicle. Any driver who receives a fixed-penalty notice (yellow or white) can elect to have the matter dealt with by a court to defend himself or to put forward mitigating circumstances. Alternatively he can accept guilt and pay the penalty. However, failure to pay within the requisite period (twenty eight days) will result in the penalties being increased by 50%. In this case the increased amount becomes a fine and non-payment will lead to arrest and a court appearance.

Offences include-:

Yellow Ticket (endorsable)

- Speeding.
- Contravention of motorway regulations.
- Defective vehicle components (brakes, steering, tyres) and vehicle in a dangerous condition.
- Contravention of traffic signs.
- Insecure and dangerous loads.
- Leaving vehicles in dangerous positions.
- Contravention of pedestrian rights.

White ticket (non-endorsable)

- Not wearing seat belt.
- Driving and stopping offences (reversing, parking, towing).
- Contravention of traffic signs, box junctions, bus lanes.
- Contravening driving prohibitions.
- Vehicle defects (brakes, steering, speedometer, wipers).
- Contravening exhaust and noise regulations.
- Exceeding weight limits (overloading).

- Contravention of vehicle lighting requirements.
- Contravention of vehicle excise requirements.

This is only a summary of an extensive list of offences. Failure to pay a fixed penalty within the prescribed period can result in a fine unless a statutory statement of ownership or of fact (to the effect that he was not the legal owner of the vehicle at the time the alleged offence was committed or that, if he was the owner, the vehicle was being used without his permission) has been given to the police in whose area the original offence was committed.

Prosecution

Where one of the following road traffic offences is committed, the offender must be warned of possible prosecution at the time (unless an accident occurred at that time or immediately after wards) or alternatively, within fourteen days, must be served with either a Notice of Intended Prosecution or a summons for the offence:-

- • Dangerous, careless, inconsiderate driving.
- • Failure to comply with traffic signs or the directions of a police con stable on traffic duty.
- • Leaving a vehicle in a dangerous position.
- • Notice of Intended Prosecution

The Notice of Intended Prosecution must be in writing and must specify the offence, the time, and place committed. It must be served on the driver who committed the offence or the registered keeper of the vehicle. If, after due diligence, the police are unable to trace the vehicle driver or registered keeper within fourteen days, action can still be taken to bring about a prosecution. If, as a result of the offence (or immediately after the offence was committed), an accident occurs, there is no requirement to serve a Notice of Intended Prosecution.

The Summons

In the case of offences other than those listed, such as those committed immediately before or at the time of an accident, a summons (to answer the charges before the court) should normally be issued within six months of the date of the offence but in the case of certain offences (obtaining a driving licence while disqualified; driving while disqualified; using an uninsured vehicle; forging a driving licence or test and insurance certificates or making false statements in connection with driving licences, test and insurance certificates) proceedings may be brought for up to three years.

The summons will give details of the offence including when and where it took place. The court to hear the case will be named within six months. The recipient of a summons must respond as follows:-

- appear in court in person on the appointed day and make a plea of guilty or not guilty

- appoint a legal representative to appear in court and make a plea on his behalf

- plead guilty in writing to the court and allow the case to be heard in his absence (in certain cases the court may adjourn the hearing and summon the defendant to appear in person)

A not guilty plea will not (cannot) be accepted in writing. The offender must surrender his driving licence when required to do so to the court, either by delivering it in person or by sending it by post to arrive on the day prior to the hearing or by having it with him at the hearing. Failure to do so is an offence and the licence will be suspended from the time its production was required and until it is produced (thus to continue driving with it is a further offence). Where a person fails to produce his licence to the court as required, the police will request its production and will seize it and hand it over to the court.

Court Hearing

Depending on the nature of the offence, the court may hear the case in the absence of the offender and accept a written plea of guilty with a statement of mitigating circumstances. Alternatively, the hearing may be suspended pending the personal appearance of the offender. Following the hearing, a verdict will be reached. If the offender is judged not guilty the matter is ended.

If the offender is found guilty, a summary conviction is made. If the case concerns an indictable offence (one which must be tried before a jury) the accused may be bailed or remanded for the case to be heard by the Crown Court. On conviction (indictment) by the court, a penalty will be imposed (a fine or imprisonment or both) as appropriate. The driver may be disqualified from driving or have his licence endorsed with an appropriate number of penalty points.

Where an offence requires obligatory disqualification under the Road Traffic Offenders Act 1988, 34{1} but for special reasons the court decides not to impose that penalty it must, as an alternative, endorse a penalty of four points on the offender's driving licence. Further offences under the Road Traffic Act 1988 allow the courts a discretionary power of disqualification with the alternative of the obligatory endorsement of a specified number of penalty points on the offender's licence.

12-point Disqualification

The penalty points system does not alter the mandatory disqualification procedure on conviction for serious offences. Also, disqualification of the driving licence will automatically follow, for a minimum of six months, when twelve or more penalty points are accrued in a period of three years counting from the date of the first offence to the current offence and not from the date of conviction.

Subsequent Disqualifications

When a driver has been disqualified once, any subsequent disqualifications within three years (preceding the date of the latest offence - not conviction) will be for progressively longer periods.

The court has discretion to disqualify for a period of less than the normal six-month minimum or not to disqualify when twelve points are endorsed on a licence in exceptional circumstances but in such cases it is required to endorse the driving licence with four penalty points.

Special Reasons for Non-Disqualification

The court has discretion in exceptional mitigating circumstances not to impose an obligatory disqualification. However, the mitigating circumstances must not be of a nature which appears to make the offence not serious, and no account must be taken of hardship other than exceptional hardship. Furthermore, if account has previously been taken of circumstances in mitigation of a disqualification, the same circumstance cannot be considered again within three years.

Other Reasons for Non-Disqualification

Where a person is convicted of an offence requiring obligatory disqualification and he can prove to the court that he did not know and had no reasonable cause to suspect that his actions would result in an offence being committed, the court must not disqualify him or order any penalty points to be endorsed on his driving licence.

Removal of Disqualification

Disqualifications may be removed from a driving licence after the following periods:-

- If disqualification for less than four years - after two years.
- If disqualification for four years to ten years - after half the period.
- If disqualification for more than ten years - after five years.

Penalty Points System (not applicable in Northern Ireland)

When drivers are convicted of offences where the court has discretion about imposing a disqualification but is obliged to endorse a licence, the endorsement takes the form of a number of penalty points. The number of points varies according to a scale ranging from two to ten points depending on the seriousness of the offence (as specified in Schedule 2 of the Road Traffic Offenders Act 1988). When the court convicts a driver of more than one offence at the same hearing, only the points relative to the most serious of the offences will be endorsed - the points relative to each individual offence will not be aggregated.

Removal of Penalty Points. If a driver is convicted for an offence and is disqualified from driving, any existing penalty points on the licence will be erased. The driver will then start again with a "clean slate" except that subsequent disqualifications will be for a longer period.

When the time interval between one endorsement on a licence and a subsequent endorsement is greater than three years (from the date of each offence), the earlier points no longer count towards disqualification.

Penalty-point endorsements (and disqualifications) shown on driving licences can be removed by applying for the issue of a new licence after the following periods of time:-

- For disqualifications and offences other than those below - fter four years from the date of the offence (from the date of conviction in the case of a disqualification).
- For reckless driving offences - after four years from the date of conviction.
- For drink-driving offences - after eleven years.

DRIVER'S PROTECTION MANUAL

SEVEN

ACCIDENTS - DON'T GET BLAMED, DO THE RIGHT THING

There will be the occasional time when you are involved in a road traffic accident. Sometimes the police will be called and other times not. The important thing to remember is that there are certain steps that needs to be taken whether or not a police officer is on the scene.

If the police are called to the scene of a road traffic accident, the officer will take down details of what he sees at the scene. He may well take down witness statements and make notes of explanations given by the drivers of both vehicles. It is quite likely that the officer may take photos of the accident scene depending on whether it is a major accident or a minor one. There will then be an ensuing period during which the police will decide if there has been any breach of the law and who was at fault, they will then make a decision as to whether or not to prosecute.

It is of course important not to admit responsibility for any kind of road accident. This should be an absolute rule that applies 100% of the time. The reason for this is that following an accident the drivers concerned, as well as their passengers, may frequently be suffering some degree of trauma and unable to form a clear account as to what happened. They may blame themselves or they may blame the other driver. In either case the blame could be entirely wrong and prejudice any future case, both for insurance claims and for possible future court action. Therefore literally say nothing that may implicate you in any blame whatsoever.

During the ensuing period you will then have time to recount the details of what happened, possibly revisiting the scene of the accident, looking at photographs that you took at the time, drawing a plan of the road, writing down details of the road conditions at the time in terms of weather, amount of traffic and visibility. (It is always a good idea to have a camera in your glove compartment.) There is a good chance that you will not need this information, as quite often the police will not prosecute in accidents where there has been no injury to people. However, this is impossible to gauge at the time and once again as much information as you can possibly gather both then and subsequently may well prove to be a lifesaver.

Typical charges that can be applied by the police following an accident would be driving without due care and attention, or careless driving. This can be a very grey area within the motoring courts and a driver who appears in court to oppose such a charge, well armed with information, stands a good chance of overturning the case. The whole case of careless driving depends on the police interpretation of the circumstances at the time, and this is very much a matter of opinion in a great number of cases, probably the majority. Therefore a very informed and spirited defence against this charge is likely to overturn it. Here are the main rules and regulations, as they apply to both private and commercial vehicles:-

Employers, self-employed operators and, where relevant, employees are required by law to report certain accidents as follows:-

- road traffic accidents causing personal injury
- damage to vehicles, animals or property under the Road Traffic Act 1988
- industrial/works accidents causing death or more than three days' incapacity for work under RIDDOR (The Reporting of Injuries, Diseases and Dangerous Occurrences Regulations 1995)

In the event that you have an accident, what does the law require?

Whether you have been driving for years or have only been driving for a short time, an accident is likely to be a traumatic event.

Should you find yourself involved in an accident please adhere to the following procedures to make sure that you do not end up breaking the law:-

If you are the driver of a vehicle which has been involved in a road-traffic accident (RTA) and if at least one of the following circumstances has arisen then: -

you must both:-

- stop at the scene of the accident remaining there for a reasonable period of time
- give your registration number, your full name and address (or those of the owner of the vehicle is not yourself) to any persons given the nature of the accident who has reasonable grounds to ask for them

139

These circumstances are:-

- person/s other than yourself have been injured
- damage has been caused to another vehicle or to somebody else's property
- an animal has been injured or killed that is not within your own vehicle or trailer (the definition of an animal in these situations is any horse, cattle, ass, mule, sheep, pig, goat or dog)
- if you are unable to exchange the details at the scene, you are required to report the accident either at a police station or to a police constable within twenty four hours
- if another person has been injured then you must also produce your valid certificate of insurance should anyone at the scene of the accident have reasonable grounds to see it (if this is not possible you may be required to take this information to the nominated police station within seven days of the incident)

You are are not only obliged to follow these procedures if you have been directly involved in the accident, but also if your 'vehicle's presence was a factor'. As this may be open to a certain level of interpretation it may well be advisable to complete the aforementioned steps as soon as you are able. A failure to comply with these obligations could mean that up to two different offences have been committed:-

- failing to stop at the scene of the accident
- failing to report an accident
- The penalties that can be incurred for each offence include:-
- maximum fine of £5000 and
- up to ten penalty points

The court also has the power to disqualify you from driving for either offence, and if both offences are committed at the same incident is likely to do so, although circumstances will be taken on a case by case basis.

   You should also report the accident to your insurance company within a reasonable period of time. A failure to do this could give them the right to refuse you cover in the future.

Accident Prevention

Road traffic accidents involving goods vehicles are mainly caused by:-

- driving too fast
- driving while tired, unwell or under the influence of drink or drugs
- driving too close to the vehicle in front, especially on motorways "tailgating"
- turning across the path of other vehicles
- not signalling intentions (or signalling too late)
- careless overtaking
- driving a defective vehicle (inadequate brakes, steering, tyres, lights/signals)
- overloading

Assessing the Risks

It is the statutory duty of road haulage employers under health and safety legislation to assess the risks faced by their employees in loading, unloading and particularly driving goods vehicles. These risks would include:-

- people being struck or run over by vehicles manoeuvring in premises
- people falling from vehicles while loading, unloading, roping and sheeting
- drivers slipping while entering or alighting from vehicle cabs and load areas
- maintenance staff being injured while working on or beneath vehicle and trailers
- injuries caused by loads falling from vehicles and fork-lift trucks during loading and unloading
- drivers speeding/taking insufficient care on the road
- drivers reversing without assistance to guide them

Risk Prevention

Steps must be taken to reduce the identified risks by establishing suitable procedures covering the following:-

- policies on drinking and drug taking
- safety controls and monitoring
- accident/incident reporting
- accident/risk awareness
- safety information
- training and retraining

EIGHT

ADDITIONAL INFORMATION FOR MOTORCYCLISTS

In general, the rules for motorcyclists are the same as for car drivers, as far as traffic offences are concerned, e.g. speeding, driving without due care etc. Some local parking regulations are different, you will need to check with your local authority to see what these are and how they apply to you.

Where there are essential differences, these are with regards to licensing requirements and some laws unique to motorcycles, such as the requirement to wear a protective helmet. Here are the laws as they apply currently.

To ride a motorcycle on the road you must be at least 17 years old (16 for a moped) and gave a driving licence which allows you to ride motorcycles. This is a category A license.

If you have a provisional motorcycle licence or a full car licence you may ride motorcycles up to 125cc and 11kW power output, with L plates, on public roads. To obtain your full motorcycle licence you

MUST pass a motorcycle theory test and then a practical test.

If you have a full moped licence and wish to obtain full motorcycle entitlement you will be required to take a motorcycle theory test if you did not take a separate theory test when you obtained your moped licence. You must then pass a practical motorcycle test.

Light motorcycle licence (A1):

- you must take a test on a motorcycle of between 75 and 120cc
- if you pass you may ride a motorcycle up to 125cc with power output up to 11Kw

Standard motorcycle licence (A):

- if your test vehicle is between 120 and 125cc and capable of more than 62 mph (100 km/h) you will be given a standard (A) licence
- you will then be restricted to motorcycles of up to 25 kW for two years, not counting any periods of disqualification or revocation
- after two years you may ride any size of machine

You must not carry a pillion passenger or pull a trailer until you have passed your test.

A moped must have an engine capacity not exceeding 50cc, not weigh more than 250kg and be designed to have a maximum speed not exceeding 31mph (50km/h).

From June 2003 all EC Type Approved mopeds have been restricted to 28mph (45km/h).

To ride a moped, learners must be 16 or over and have a provisional moped licence.

You must first pass the theory test for motorcycles and then the moped practical test to obtain your full moped licence.

If you have a full car licence or motorcycle licence you are qualified to ride a moped without L plates.

Note. For motorcycle and moped riders wishing to upgrade, the following gives exemption from taking the motorcycle theory test:

- a full A1 motorcycle licence gained on or after 1 January 1997
- a full moped licence gained on or after 1 July 1996

All learner motorcyclists and moped riders must complete CBT before riding on the road unless they:

- Passed a full moped test after 1 December 1990 Live and ride on specified Offshore islands
- Already hold a Certificate of Completion (DL196) obtained during a previous motorcycle entitlement or when riding a mopedIntend to ride a moped and passed the car tests before 1st Feb 2001

You need to take a multiple choice test of about 35 questions lasting about 30-40 minutes, complete with a series of video clips where a candidate must pick out developing hazards. Since 1 February 2001, anyone wishing to take a motorcycle test must pass the theory test before they can book the practical test. There is no exemption for car licence holders. The Theory pass certificate is valid for 2 years.

When you've completed CBT you'll be given a DL196. You must produce this before you can take the practical motorcycle test. A DL196 has a 2 year life. If you don't pass both your theory and practical tests in that time then you'll have to take the CBT course again.

A DL196 obtained on a moped is valid for a motorcycle when the rider reaches the age of

There are three types of full motorcycle licence.

1. Category P - moped.

2. Category A1 - light motorcycle licence - to receive this you must take and pass your test on a motorcycle with an engine size over 75cc but not more than 125cc, a power output of not more than 11kW (14.6 bph) and, a maximum speed of not more than 100 kph (62.5 mph). You will now have full licence entitlement on any motorcycle up to 125cc and with a power output of up to 11kW (14.6 bhp). This licence is intended for riders of small motorcycles and scooters who don't intend to ride anything bigger. It will not become an unrestricted category A licence after two years. If you take a test on a small motorcycle then you will have to take another test to ride anything bigger than a 125cc, 11kW bike with a maximum speed of over 100kph (62.5mph).

3. Category A - standard motorcycle licence - (aka A2) - this is what you'll obtain if you pass your test on a motorcycle over 120cc but not over 125cc and is capable of more than 100 kph (62.5mph). With this licence you are entitled to ride a motorcycle up to 25kW (33 bhp) and a power to weight ratio not exceeding 0.16kw/kg.

There is no restriction on engine size (cc) so you can now ride a bike bigger than a 125cc. There are plenty of bikes around in the 125cc to 400cc range that produce no more than 25kW (33bhp). You can ride a bike with a power output over 25kW but you'll need a restrictor kit on it to restrict the power output to 25kW. Any good motorcycle mechanic will fit a restrictor for you and give you the necessary documentation. Your insurance will cost more though because insurance companies tend to disregard restrictors.

If your practical test is passed on an automatic motorcycle the full licence gained will be restricted to automatic bikes only.

Learners who wish to ride with a sidecar can practice on a combination with a power/weight ratio not exceeding 0.16 kW/kg. On obtaining a standard licence, you will be restricted to a combination with the same power/weight ratio for two years. At age 21 learners may, only within direct or accelerated access, practice on a larger combination, but the test must be taken on a solo bike (although physically disabled riders can use a combination).

MOTORCYCLE DOCUMENTS

The Registration Document (VRD) - this contains details of your motorcycle

*Make and model*Year of first registration*Engine size and number

It also gives your name and address.

If you buy a new motorcycle the dealer will register it with the DVLA. A registration document will then be sent directly to you from the DVLA.

If you buy a second-hand one you'll receive the VRD from the seller. Fill in the "Change of ownership" section and send it to the DVLA at the address given on the document. You should do this immediately as it is an offence not to notify the DVLA.

Vehicle excise duty

Also known as the 'vehicle licence' or 'road tax'. You must display the 'tax disc' on the vehicle.

You can get the vehicle licence application form at any post office and most main post offices can accept your application.

The fee varies with engine size. The classes are

*Not over 150cc*Over 150cc up to 400cc*Over 400cc up to 600cc*All other motorcycles

When you apply to renew your vehicle excise licence you must produce:

1. A vehicle test certificate (MOT) if your motorcycle is three years old and overb.

2. A valid certificate of insurance.

3. An excise licence renewal form

Older motorcycles

Motorcycles registered before 1st of January 1973 are exempt from tax but should display a tax free (historic) disc.

The MOT test applies to all motorcycles, mopeds and scooters over 3 years old. The test must be carried out every year at an appointed vehicle testing station. The purpose of the test is to check that your motorcycle is roadworthy. When your machine passes the test you'll be given a vehicle test certificate which you'll need to produce when you renew your vehicle excise licence. If your motorcycle fails the test you must not ride it on the road unless you're taking it to have the faults corrected or unless you're taking it for an arranged retest.

It's illegal to ride without insurance. Before you take a motorcycle onto public roads you must get proper insurance cover. Insurance costs depend mostly on your age, the size of the bike and the area where you live. One of the UK market leaders for motorcycle insurance is Bennetts. To get an online quote please click on the banner below. You can save the quote they give you so you don't have to complete the form again if you go back later.

By law, you must wear a safety helmet when riding a motorcycle on the road. All helmets sold in the UK must either comply with British Standard BS 6658:1985 and carry the BSI kitemark or comply with UNECE

Regulation 22.05 or comply with any standard accepted by a member of the European Economic Area which offers a level of safety and protection equivalent to BS 6658:1985 and carry a mark equivalent to the BSI kitemark.

You must ensure at all times that your motorcycle or moped is road legal and that it has a valid MOT (Ministry of Transport) certificate. Without this MOT certificate the motorbike is not classified and is therefore not legally allowed to be driven on roads. Being in charge of a motorbike or moped that does not have a valid MOT certificate is a criminal offence could result in a hefty fine or having your motorcycle or moped confiscated.

You must ensure also that all lights, tyres, mirrors and electrical elements of your vehicle are fit for purpose.

Again an important rule when purchasing such a vehicle – especially if it is classed as 'used' – is to have someone with a degree of experience accompany you. Avoid purchasing vehicles which have short periods of MOT remaining or do not have a logbook (V5).

You should not drive your motorcycle on a motorway if you are not licensed to do so. You are only permitted to drive a motorcycle on a motorway upon successfully passing your practical test. If you are found to be breaking this law you can be fined and have the vehicle confiscated.

As a learner rider it is your responsibility to ensure that the aforementioned are carried out and carried out correctly within the legal requirements. You should be aware that any failure to do so could delay or prevent you from taking your practical test and getting out onto the open road legally.

As previously stated, on all journeys, the rider and pillion passenger on a motorcycle, scooter or moped must wear a protective helmet. This does not apply to a follower of the Sikh religion while wearing a turban. Helmets must comply with the Regulations and they must be fastened securely. Riders and passengers of motor tricycles and quadricycles, also called quadbikes, should also wear a protective helmet. Before each journey check that your helmet visor is clean and in good condition. It is also advisable to wear eye protectors, which must comply with the Regulations. Scratched or poorly fitting eye protectors can limit your view when riding, particularly in bright sunshine and the hours of darkness. Consider wearing ear protection. Strong boots, gloves and suitable clothing may help to protect you if you are involved in a collision.

You must not carry more than one pillion passenger who must sit astride the machine on a proper seat. They should face forward with both feet on the footrests. You must not carry a pillion passenger unless your motor cycle is designed to do so. Provisional licence holders must not carry a pillion passenger.

Here are some additional notes to keep yourself alive and in one piece.

Make yourself as visible as possible from the side as well as the front and rear. You could wear a light or brightly coloured helmet and fluorescent clothing or strips. Dipped headlights, even in good daylight, may also make you more conspicuous. However, be aware that other vehicle drivers may still not have seen you, or judged your distance or speed correctly, especially at junctions.

Wear reflective clothing when riding in the dark, or strips to improve your visibility in the dark. These reflect light from the headlamps of other vehicles, making you visible from a longer distance. You should be aware of what is behind and to the sides before manoeuvring. Look behind you; use mirrors if they are fitted. When in traffic queues look out for pedestrians crossing between vehicles and vehicles emerging from junctions or changing lanes. Position yourself so that drivers in front can see you in their mirrors. Additionally, when filtering in slow-moving traffic, take care and keep your speed low.

DRIVER'S PROTECTION MANUAL

GLOSSARY

A

Accused

The person charged. The person who has allegedly committed the offence

Acknowledgement of service

When the particulars of a claim form (outlining details of the claim) are served on (delivered to) a defendant, they receive a response pack including a form which they must use to acknowledge they have received the claim. The defendant must file (return) the

acknowledgment form within 14 days of receiving the particulars of the claim. The particulars can be served with, or separately from the claim form.

Acquittal

Discharge of defendant following verdict or direction of not guilty

Act

Law, as an act of parliament

Adjourned generally or sine die

Temporary suspension of the hearing of a case by order of the Court (maybe for a short period, e.g. to next day or sine die).

Adjournment

the postponing of the hearing of a case until a later date.

Adjudication

153

A judgment or decision of a court, tribunal or adjudicator in alternative dispute resolution (ADR) cases where disputes are resolved outside of the court

Administrative Court

the Administrative Court is part of the High Court. It deals with applications for judicial review.

Administration order

An order by a County Court directing a debtor to pay a specified monthly installment into Court in respect of outstanding debts. The Court retains the payments made and at intervals distributes it between the creditors on a pro-rata basis

Admission (including part admissions)

A party involved in a claim may admit the truth of all or part of the other party's case, at any stage during proceedings. For example, a defendant may agree that he or she owes some money, but less than the amount being claimed. If the defendant makes an admission, the claimant may apply for judgment, on the admission.

Advocate

A barrister or solicitor representing a party in a hearing before a Court

Adversarial Amendment

The process by which corrections to court documents, such as statements of case, can be made. A statement of case can be amended at any time, before it is served or with permission of all other parties or the court, (once served). The court may reject the

amendment, even if the party concerned has permission of other parties to the case

Amount offered in satisfaction

An amount of money offered by a defendant to pay a debt or to settle another type of claim, for example in a personal injury case

Annul

To declare no longer valid

Appeal

Application to a higher court or other body for review of a decision taken by a lower court or tribunal. The higher court may overturn or uphold (i.e. reject) the lower court's decision. Often, permission (leave) is required, to for an appeal to occur.

Appellant

A person appealing to a higher court or body against a decision made in a lower court or body

Applicant

Person making the request or demand, e.g. person who issues an application

Application

The act of applying to a civil court to ask it to do something, for example to start proceedings

Appraisement or appraisal

Valuation of goods seized under warrant of execution prior to sale

Apportioning

To place or assign

Appraisement or appraisal

Valuation of goods seized under warrant of execution prior to sale

Arbitrator or Arbitration

A process in which both sides agree to use an independent arbitrator (an impartial person) who gives a binding decision in the matter. The person making the claim (claimant) has to choose between going to arbitration and court – it is not usually possible to take a claim to court after it has been through arbitration

Assisted person (legally)

A party to legal proceedings who is receiving legal aid

Attachment of earnings order

An order that instructs an employer to deduct a regular amount, fixed by the court, from a debtor's earnings and to pay that money into court. The court pays the money to the person or people to whom it is owed

Automatic transfer

Providing that a number of criteria are met, proceedings must be transferred automatically to the court nearest to the defendant's home.

Award

Result of an arbitration hearing or the amount of damages assessed by a Court

B

Bail

Release of a defendant from custody, until his/her next appearance in Court, subject sometimes to security being given and/or compliance with certain conditions

Bailiff

Bailiffs and enforcement officers are people authorised to remove and sell possessions in order to pay the money a debtor owes to a person or an organisation. They may also conduct evictions, and arrest people. A bailiff can also serve (deliver) court documents on people

Bankrupt

Insolvent - unable to pay creditors and having all goods/effects administered by a liquidator or trustee and sold for the benefit of those creditors; as a result of an order under the Insolvency Act 1986

Bar

The collective term for barristers

Barrister

(see Counsel; Silk) A member of the bar: a lawyer entitled to represent clients in all the courts

Bench warrant

A warrant issued by the judge for an absent defendant to be arrested and brought before a Court

Bill of costs

(see Taxation of costs, Summary assessment and Detailed assessment.

Bill of indictment

A written statement of the charges against a defendant sent for trial to the Crown Court, and signed by an officer of the Court

Bind over

In the Crown Court or (more usually) the Magistrates Court, and signed by an officer of the Court

Bind over for sentence

An order which requires the defendant to return to Court on an unspecified date for sentence. Failure to observe this order may result in a forfeit or penalty to be enforced

Bound / binding

A binding decision is one that must be obeyed by the people concerned. For example, it is not possible to go to court after a binding decision has been issued by an arbitrator

Brief

Written instructions to counsel to appear at a hearing on behalf of a party prepared by the solicitor and setting out the facts of the case and any case law relied upon

Business address

Premises or place from which business activities take place

C

Case

An action, suit or claim in a court of law. It can also mean the arguments put forward by parties in a court of law

Case disposal

The case is taken out of the court process (see Disposal).

Case Management Conference (CMC)

This is a meeting between all parties to a case and the Judge to check the progress of the case, with regards to costs and other matters. The numbers of CMCs held depend on the complexity of the case

Case management tracks

Civil cases are allocated to one of three case management

tracks, depending on financial value, issues of law and the likely duration (length) of the case. The three tracks are (i) the small claims track in which cases to the value of five thousand pounds can be considered and the claimant does not have to have legal representation (ii) the fast track for cases of value between five and fifteen thousand pounds and (iii) the multi- track for cases of value over fifteen thousand pounds. Legal representation is advisable in the fast and multi-tracks

Case number

A unique reference number allocated to each case by the issuing Court

Case value

The financial value of a case - known as case value - is one of the factors used to asses which track a case (claim) should be allocated to.

Caution

Warning, given by a Police Officer, to a person charged with an offence

iii) Warning, given by a Police Officer, instead of a charge

Certificate of Legal Aid Costs

A certificate of costs allowed following taxation by a judicial or taxing officer (Previously referred to as an Allocatur)

Certificate of service

A document stating the date and manner in which the parties were served (given) a document. For example where a claim form is served by the claimant court rule requires the claimant to file a certificate of service within seven days of service of the claim form otherwise he may not obtain judgment in default.

Cessate

A grant of representation of limited duration which has ceased and expired

Chambers

i) Private room, or Court from which the public are excluded in which a District Judge or Judge may conduct certain sorts of hearings

ii) Offices used by a barrister

Charge

A formal accusation against a person that a criminal offence has been committed (see also Charging order)

Charging Order

A court order directing that a charge be put on the judgment debtors' property, such as a house or piece of land to secure payment of money due. This prevents the debtor from selling the property or land - without paying what is owed to the claimant

Circuit Judge

A judge between the level of a High Court Judge and a District Judge, who sits in the County Court and/or Crown Court

Citizen's Advice Bureau

(CAB)

A charity which can offer free legal and financial advice to the general public.

Civil

Matters concerning private rights and not offences against the state

Civil case or claim

A civil dispute that involves court action.

Civil Justice or civil law

A branch of the law which applies to the rights and dealings of private citizens, (including such matters as unpaid debts, negligence and the enforcement of contracts). It does not include criminal, immigration, employment or family matters

Civil Procedure

The rules and procedures to be followed for civil cases in the county courts and High Court

Civil Procedure Rules

The rules and procedures for proceedings in civil courts England and Wales. An important feature is active case management by the courts.

Claim

Proceedings issued in the County or High Court. Previously know as an Action.

Claimant

The person issuing the claim. Previously known as the Plaintiff

Claim form

Proceedings in a civil court start with the issuing of a claim form. The form, which is issued by the court (after the claimant has filed the form in court), includes a summary of the nature of the claim and the remedy (compensation or amends) sought

Coercion

Coercion exists when an individual is forced to behave in a particular way, by threats of violence, for example. The person concerned does not act freely

Collaboration / collaborative

Working together to solve a problem

Commercial Court

Part of the Queen's Bench Division of the High Court.

Commissioner of Oaths

Solicitors authorised by the Lord Chancellor to administer oaths and affirmations to a statement of evidence

Committal

i) Committal for trial: Following examination by the Magistrates of a case involving and indictable or either way offence, the procedure of directing the case to the Crown Court to be dealt with

ii) Committal for Sentence: Where the Magistrates consider that the offence justifies a sentence greater than they are empowered to impose they may commit the defendant to the Crown Court for sentence to be passed by a judge

iii) Committal Order: An order of the Court committing someone to prison

iv) Committal Warrant (see WARRANT OF COMMITTAL)

Common Law

The law established, by precedent, from judicial decisions and established within a community

Compensation

Usually a sum of money offered in recompense (to make amends) for an act, error or omission that harmed someone. The harm suffered may have been loss, personal injury or inconvenience

Complainant

A person who makes a complaint

Complaint

Expressing discontent for something

Concurrent Sentence

A direction by a Court that a number of sentences of imprisonment should run at the same time

Concurrent Writ

A duplicate of the original writ bearing the same date and expiring at the same time as the original

Conditional Discharge

A discharge of a convicted defendant without sentence on condition that he/she does not re-offend within a specified period of time

Conduct Money

i) Money paid to a witness in advance of the hearing of a case as compensation for time spent attending Court ii) Commonly used to describe expenses paid to a debtor to cover the costs of traveling to Court

Consecutive Sentence

An order for a subsequent sentence of imprisonment to commence as soon as a previous sentence expires. Can apply to more than two sentences

Contempt of Court

Disobedience or wilful disregard to the judicial process.   In civil cases, for example, failing to appear as a witness without informing the court or the party that called you. A person found to be in civil contempt of court could be fined.

Contents of trial (civil)

see trial contents

Contributory Negligence

Partial responsibility of a claimant for the injury in respect of which he/she claims damages

Corroboration

Evidence by one person confirming that of another or supporting evidence, for example forensic evidence (bloodstain, fibres etc) in murder cases

Costs (civil)

In civil proceedings the general rule is the person who wins the case is entitled to his or her costs. The court may decide to reduce the costs to be paid by the losing side if it feels that the winner has behaved unreasonably. The award of costs is at the court's discretion

Counsel

A Barrister or solicitor in legal proceedings

Count

An individual offence set out in an indictment

Counterclaim

A claim made by a defendant against a claimant in an action. There is no limit imposed on a counterclaim, but a fee is payable according to the amount counterclaimed

County Court

County courts deal with civil matters such as disputes over contracts, unpaid debts and negligence claims. County courts deal with all monetary claims up to £50,000. There are 218 county courts in England and Wales. The county court is a court of the first instance – where civil cases start

County court judgment (CCJ)

A judgment of the county court that orders a defendant to pay a sum of money to the claimant. CCJs are recorded on the Register of County Court Judgments for six years and can affect a defendant's ability to borrow money

Court

Body with judicial powers (see also Courtroom)

Court of Appeal

Divided into:

i) civil and

ii) criminal divisions and hears appeals:

i) from decisions in the High Court and county courts and,

ii) against convictions or sentences passed by the Crown Court, (see also Public trustee Monies held in Court, in the name of the Accountant General, for suitors, minors, Court of Protection patients etc)

Court fees

The County Court will charge to issue a claim in a civil case and to launch enforcement proceedings if the defendant ignores the judgment of the court. You will also be charged if you make applications to the court

Courtroom

The room in which cases are heard

Covenant

A formal agreement or a contract constituting an obligation to perform an act

Creditor

A person to whom money is owed by a debtor

Criminal

Person who has been found guilty of a criminal offence

Cross-examination

The questioning of a witness for the other side in a case.

Crown Court

The Crown Court deals with all crime committed for trial by Magistrates Courts. Cases for trial are heard before a judge and jury. The Crown Court also acts as an appeal Court for cases heard and dealt with by the Magistrates. The Crown Court can also deal with some civil and family matters.

Magistrates' Court.

Third Tier

Class 4 offences only in criminal proceedings.

Committals for sentence from Magistrates' Court.

Appeals against convictions and sentences.

D

Damages

An amount of money claimed as compensation for physical/ material loss, e.g. personal injury, breach of contract

Date of service (civil

claims)

The date of service of the claim is the date upon which the defendant receives the claim form issued by the court on behalf of the claimant. If the 'particulars of claim' section is completed or the particulars of claim are attached, the defendant must acknowledge receipt within 14 days

Debt recovery after judgment - See Enforcement

Debtor

A person who owes money to someone or to an organisation

Decree

An order of the Court in proceedings commenced by petition

Declaration

Court order setting out the rights of a party in the form of a statement

Deed

A legal document which sets out the terms of an agreement, which is signed by both parties

Default Judgment

May be obtained without a hearing by the claimant if the defendant fails to reply or pay within a 14 day period after service of the claim. A claimant can apply for a default judgment if the amount claimed is specified or for a judgment on liability if the amount claimed is unspecified.

Defence or defending a claim (civil)

When the defendant disputes the claim made by the claimant

Defendant (civil)

The person who has a claim made against them. They can defend (dispute the claim) or admit liability, in part or in full

Defendant (criminal)

Person standing trial or appearing for sentence

Deponent

Person giving evidence by affidavit

Deposition

A statement of evidence written down and sworn on oath, or by affirmation

Designated Civil Judge

A Judge designated to deal with the Civil Justice Reforms for a group of courts

Detailed Assessment (of costs)

When a court makes a costs order it may make a detailed assessment of costs, usually at the conclusion of proceedings. A costs officer would carry out the assessment.

Determination (criminal)

Act of scrutinising a bill of costs in criminal proceedings to see if the work done and amount claimed is reasonable

Determination (civil)

If the defendant offers to pay to the claimant an amount by instalments and the claimant refuses the offer, an officer of the court will make an assessment of what would be reasonable for the defendant to pay

Directions (civil)

case management instructions given by the judge which give a time-table for pre-trial procedures. In cases allocated to the small claims track the judge will usually give standard directions, in cases allocate to the multi-track, there may be several hearings on directions

Disability

The inability of a person to handle their own affairs (e.g. through mental illness or a minor under 18 years of age) which prevents involvement in civil legal proceedings without representation

Disclosure

Parties to a civil case must disclose (show to the other party) documents they intend to rely on in court to support their case

Discovery of documents

(see INSPECTION OF DOCUMENTS) Mutual exchange of evidence and all relevant information held by each party relating to the case

Discontinuance

Notice given by the Court, on instruction by the claimant, that they no longer wish to proceed with the case

Dismissal

To make order or decision that a claim be ceased

Disposal

See Case disposal

Dispute

A civil problem not dealt with in court, (a civil dispute which comes to court is called a civil case); challenging the views of the opposing party in a civil case

District Judge

A judicial officer of the Court whose duties involve hearing applications made within proceedings and final hearings subject to any limit of jurisdiction Previously known as Registrars

District Registry

see High Court

Divisional Court

As well as having an original jurisdiction of their own, all three divisions of the High Court have appellate jurisdiction to hear appeals from lower Courts and tribunals. The Divisional Court of the Chancery Division deals with appeals in bankruptcy matters from the County Court. The Divisional Court of the Queen's Bench Division deals largely with certain appeals on points of law from many Courts. The Divisional Court of the Family Division deals largely with appeals from Magistrates Courts in matrimonial matters a 'next friend' or 'guardian ad litem'

Dock

Enclosure in criminal Court for the defendant on trial

E

Either-way Offence

(see Indictable Offence, Summary Offence) An offence for which the accused may elect the case to be dealt with either summarily by the magistrates or by committal to the Crown Court to be tried by jury

Enforcement

Method of pursuing a civil action after judgment has been made in favour of a party. Process carried out by Magistrates Court to collect fines and other monetary orders made in the Crown Court

Enforcement / enforcing a judgment

When a judgment/order has not been paid or terms obeyed with, enforcement proceedings can be issued to ensure compliance. A court can order such action as the seizure of a defendant's property for sale

Entering judgment on admission

The claimant can ask the court to enter judgment on admission when the defendant has admitted all or part of the case and offered payment or other restitution

Entry of Judgment

Decision of the Court in favour of one or other of the parties

Estate

The rights and assets of a person in property

Evidence

Documentary or other material which is used to support a person's case in a court of law

Execution

(see Levy) Seizure of debtors goods following non payment of a

Court order

Exempt

To be freed from liability or allegiance

Exhibit

Item or document referred to in an affidavit or used as evidence during a Court trial or hearing

Expert Witness

Person employed to give evidence on a subject in which they are qualified or have expertise

F

Fast Track

The path to which defended claims of not more than £15,000 are allocated.

Fiat

A decree or command

Fieri-Facias (FI-FA)

(see Sheriff) High Court version of warrant of execution in County Court. A directive by a High Court to a sheriff to seize sufficient goods of a debtor to satisfy judgment debt

Filing

The process of delivering or presenting forms and other documents to a court. For example a claim or a defence to a claim must be filed

Fixed costs

Costs in civil cases that are set at a certain level and can be claimed in specific circumstances. For example, if a defendant does not acknowledge a claim, the claimant can obtain judgment and an order for fixed costs to offset the cost of beginning the claim

G

Garnishee

A summons issued by a plaintiff, against a third party, for seizure of money or other assets in their keeping, but belonging to the defendant

Group Litigation Orders

A Group Litigation Order can be made in a claim in which there are multiple parties or claimants. The order will provide for the case management of claims which give rise to common or related issues of fact or law

Guarantor

Someone who promises to make payment for another if payment is not made by the person responsible for making the repayments of a loan or hire purchase agreement

Guardian

A person appointed to safeguard/protect/manage the interests of a child or person under mental disability (see Next Friend)

H

Hearing

A hearing is the trial of the case. Hearings are usually held in public High Court A civil Court which consists of three divisions:-

i) Queen's Bench (can be known as King's Bench Division if a King is assuming the throne) - civil disputes for recovery of money, including breach of contract, personal injuries, libel/slander;

ii) Family - concerned with matrimonial maters and proceedings relating to children, e.g. wardship;

iii) Chancery - property matters including fraud and bankruptcy

High Court Enforcement

Officers

An enforcement officer appointed by the Lord Chancellor to enforce High Court judgments and orders

Home court (civil)

The court nearest to the defendant's home or place of business

Housing claim

The procedure that a landlord may use in a county court to recover land or property (and money for arrears of rent or damage to property, if applicable).

I

Impartial

Not having or showing any favouritism to one side in a dispute

Independent

Person or organisation not connected to any of the parties in a dispute or legal case

Indictable Offence

A criminal offence triable only by the Crown Court. The different types of offence are classified 1, 2, 3 or 4. Murder is a class 1 offence

Infant

Also known as a minor: A person under 18 years of age which prevents them from acting on their own behalf in legal proceedings

Injunction

A court order which either restrains a person from a course of action or behaviour, or which requires a person to follow another course of action.

Inspection of Documents

(see Disclosure of documents) Arrangements made by the parties to allow mutual exchange and copying of documents

Instalments

A method of paying a debt in several parts at intervals. Payment by instalments is agreed to make the burden of repayment lighter

Interest

A charge for borrowed money, a percentage of the sum borrowed

Interlocutory

Interim, pending a full order/decision, e.g. interlocutory judgment for damages pending further hearing to assess amount to be awarded and entered as final judgment

Interpleader

A claim by a third party to ownership of goods levied upon under a warrant of execution which is disputed by a creditor. The Court then issues an interpleader summons for the parties to attend Court to adjudicate on rightful ownership

Interim order

An order made during proceedings which is not a final order

Issue / issuing

To initiate legal proceedings in pursuit of a claim

J

Judge

An officer appointed to administer the law and who has authority to hear and try cases in a court of law

Judgment

The decision or sentence issued by a court in legal proceedings

Judgment set aside

A judgment or order can be set aside (made void) at the request of a party to the case in certain circumstances, for example if they were too ill to attend court on the day of the judgment

Judicial/Judiciary

i)   Relating to the Administration of justice or to the judgment of a Court

ii)   ii) A judge or other officer empowered to act as a judge

Judicial discretion (civil)

Judges have the power to decide how best to manage the case on the individual facts. They do not necessarily have to look at how similar cases are managed. The judge has very wide case management powers under Rule 3 of the civil procedure rules to decide on the evidence parties produce how best to manage their case

Judicial review

The High Court can review decisions of inferior (lower) courts, public bodies and other bodies to ensure that the decision making process has been lawful

Jurat

A statement contained at the conclusion of an affidavit which states the name of the person giving the evidence, the name of the person before whom and the place where the oath or affirmation was taken

Jurisdiction

The area and matters over which a court has legal authority

Juror

(see Jury) A person who has been summoned by a Court to be a member of the jury

Jury

Body of jurors sworn to reach a verdict according to the evidence in a Court

Justice of the Peace

A lay magistrate - person appointed to administer judicial business in a Magistrates Court. Also sits in the Crown Court with a judge or recorder to hear appeals and committals for sentence

Jurisdiction

The area and matters over which a Court has legal authority

Juvenile

Person under 17 years of age

L

Law

The system made up of rules established by an act of parliament, custom or practice enjoining or prohibiting certain action

Law Lords

Describes the judges of the House of Lords who are known as the

Lords of Appeal in ordinary

Lawyer

The legal profession in the UK is divided into two branches. Barristers have the right to represent clients in higher courts whereas most solicitors are restricted to represent their clients in the lower courts

Lay representative

A person, not legally qualified, who accompanies another during a court hearing. The person may be a colleague, friend or spouse.

Leading junior counsel

A senior barrister who deals with more serious cases, but not a QC.

Lease

The letting of land or tenements, e.g. rent etc, for property for a prescribed period

Leave

Leave means 'permission'. Some steps in legal action require the permission of the court. For example a losing party may be granted leave to appeal.

Legal advice

Advice about the law and your options from a qualified legal representative or advice centre

Legal Aid / Public Funding

State funded assistance, for those on low incomes, to cover legal fees.

Legal Personal Representative

The person to whom a grant of probate or letters of ADMINISTRATION has been issued

Liability

Responsibility or obligation. For example, a debt is a liability or responsibility.

Libel

A written and published statement/article which infers damaging remarks on a persons reputation

Licence

Permission to carry out an act that would otherwise be considered illegal

Lien

A legal right to withhold the goods/property of another until payment is made

Listing Questionnaire

This form is used to ensure that all issues are resolved and that the parties are ready for trial. Used for Fast track and Multi track claims only

Litigant in person

A person who starts or defends a case without legal representation. Such a person is entitled to be accompanied by another person who may advise them, but may not address the court

Litigation

Legal proceedings or court action. Litigation can be either civil or criminal proceedings.

Litigation friend

A person who conducts legal proceedings on behalf of a child or a mentally incapacitated person

Lodging

The process of filing (delivering) documents to a court.

Long Vacation

Period between 1 August and 30 September in each year during which there are only restricted High Court sittings for urgent matters

Lord Chancellor

The cabinet minister who acts as speaker of the House of Lords and oversees the hearings of the Law Lords. Additional responsibilities include supervising the procedure of Courts other than Magistrates or Coroners Courts and selection of judges, magistrates, queens counsel and members of tribunals

Lord Chief Justice

Senior judge of the Court of Appeal (Criminal Division) who also heads the Queens Bench Division of the High Court of Justice)

Lord Justice of Appeal

Title given to certain judges sitting in the Court of Appeal

M

Magistrates Court

A Court where criminal proceedings are commenced before justices of the peace who examine the evidence/statements and either deal with the case themselves or commit to the Crown Court for trial or sentence. Also has jurisdiction in a range of civil matters

Maladminstration

Maladministration is administration that leads to injustice because of such factors as excessive delay, bias or arbitrary decision-making.

Master

(see Registrar) Judicial officer of the High Court in the Royal Courts of Justice who normally deals with preliminary matters before trial

Master of the Rolls

Senior judge of the Court of Appeal (Civil Division)

Matter

(see Originating Application) Proceedings commenced by way of

originating application

Mediation

A process for resolving disagreements in which an impartial third party (the mediator) helps people in dispute to find a mutually acceptable resolution. If mediation fails court proceedings can be initiated or re-activated

Mesne Profits

Sum of money claimed by the owner of property against someone not legally entitled to be in possession. Calculated from the date the notice to quit expires until the date possession is given up

Minor

Someone below 18 years of age and unable to sue or be sued

without representation, other than for wages. A minor sues by a next friend and defends by a guardian

Mitigation

Reasons submitted on behalf of a guilty party in order to excuse or partly excuse the offence committed in an attempt to minimise the sentence

Money Claim

A claim for money only in the county court. The claim can be for a fixed on unspecified amount. See also unspecified amount of money

Money Claim Online

(MCOL)

An online Service that allows claimants to start legal proceedings which relate to money. Defendants can use the service to respond to a claim against them also

Motion

An application by one party to the High Court for an order in their favour

Multi Track

The path that defended claims over £15000 are allocated to

N

Next Friend

A person representing a minor or mental patient who is involved in legal proceedings

Non-Molestation

An order within an injunction to prevent one person physically attacking another

Non-Suit

Proceedings where the plaintiff has failed to establish to the Court's satisfaction that there is a case for the defendant to answer

Notary Public

Someone who is authorised to swear oaths and certify the execution of deeds

Notice of Issue

Notice sent by a Court to the claimant giving notification of the case number allocated to their action and details of fees paid. Confirms date of service

O

Oath

To call upon God to witness that what you say at the hearing is the truth or binding. (see affirmation)

Objection

Disagreement with an argument or set out by another at the hearing

Official Receiver

A civil servant who works for the Department of trade and Industry and is appointed by the Court to act as:-

i) a liquidator when a company is being wound up;

ii) a trustee when an individual is made bankrupt. The duties of an official receiver will include examining the company/bankrupt's property which is available to pay the debts and distributing the money amongst the creditors

Official Solicitor

A solicitor or barrister appointed by the Lord Chancellor and working in the Lord Chancellor's Department. The duties include representing, in legal proceedings, people who are incapable of looking after their own affairs i.e. children/persons suffering from mental illness

Ombudsman

Independent 'referees' who consider complaints against public and private organisations in a wide range of fields including housing, health and banking. They are often used as a last resort when complaints cannot be resolved through an organisation's own complaints procedure. Ombudsman services are free to use.

Recommendations made by ombudsmen are not binding on the

person making the complaint (complainant). They can still go to court even if the ombudsman decided against them

Oral evidence

Evidence given to a court, verbally rather than in writing

Oral Examination

A method of questioning a person under oath before an officer of the Court to obtain details of their financial affairs

Order

A direction by a Court

Oral evidence

Evidence given to a court, verbally rather than in writing

P

Part 8 Claim

An alternative procedure for issuing a claim to the court

Particulars of claim

This document contains details of the claimant's claim which must be contained in the claim form or served shortly after the claim form has been served. The particulars should be a concise statement of the facts of the claim

Party / parties

People involved in court proceedings either as the defendant(s) or claimant(s)

Party and Party

Costs that one party must pay to another

Patient

A person who is deemed incapable of handling his/her own affairs by reason of mental incapacity and who is under the jurisdiction of the Court of Protection

Penal Notice

Directions attached to an order of a Court stating the penalty for disobedience may result in imprisonment

Personal Application

Application made to the Court without legal representation

Personal injury claim

A civil claim, which relates to physical or mental harm suffered by a claimant, due to the defendant's alleged negligence

Personal Service

Personal delivery (i.e. not by mail) of a claim, summons or notice

Petition

A method of commencing proceedings whereby the order required by the petitioner from the Court is expressed as a prayer.

Petitioner

A person who presents the petition

Plaintiff

see CLAIMANT

Plaint Note

see NOTICE OF ISSUE

Plaint Number

Old-fashioned term for Claim Number

Plea

A defendant's reply to a charge put to him by a court; i.e. guilty or not guilty

Pleading Documents setting out claim/defence of parties involved in civil proceedings

Possession Claim Online

(PCOL)

An online Service which allows claimants to start legal proceedings related to property online. Defendants can use the service to respond to a claim against them also

Power of Arrest

An order attached to some injunctions to allow the police to arrest a person who has broken the terms of the order

Practice Directions

These are steps to be followed by parties to a dispute prior to legal action. The aim of the to increase co-operation between parties and therefore the chances of an early settlement

Pre-action protocols

These are steps to be followed by parties to a dispute prior to legal action. The aim is to increase co-operation between parties and therefore the chances of an early settlement

Precedent

The decision of a case which established principles of law that act as an authority for future cases of a similar nature

Preliminary hearing

A hearing in which the Judge ensures that guidance on such matters as the use of the parties understand what they must do to comply with any directions and offers an expert witness. This hearing is before the final hearing

Pre-trial checklist

A pre-trial checklist is completed before the trial. The checklist is for the parties and the Judge, as a reminder of the issues to be considered. The checklist will then be reviewed at a pre-trial review just before the final hearing.

Pre-trial Review

A meeting at which the Judge considers the issues before the timetable for the trial /final hearing date is finalised

Process

The document commencing a claim or subsequent action

Prosecution

The institution or conduct of criminal proceedings against a person

Prosecutor

Person who prosecutes (see PROSECUTION)

Public trustee

A person (usually a barrister or solicitor) appointed by the Lord Chancellor as

i) trustee for trusts managed by the Public trust Office;

ii) Accountant General for Court Funds;

iii) Receiver (of last resort) for Court of Protection patients

Puisne Judge

(Pronounced Puny) High Court judge. Any judge of the High Court other than the heads of each division. The word puisne means junior and is used to distinguish High Court judges from senior judges sitting at the Court of Appeal

Q

QC

See Queen's Counsel

Quash

To annul; i.e. to declare no longer valid

Quasi-judicial functions

A quasi-judicial function is an executive function that involves the exercise of discretion (judgment). Court staff perform quasi-judicial executive functions such as managing the issuing of claims, serving court documents and deciding what would be reasonable for the defendant to pay .

Quantum

In a damages claim the amount to be determined by the court

Queens Bench Division

A division of the High Court. The QBD has jurisdiction (reasonability for) civil disputes involving the recovery of money, including breach of contract; personal injuries; libel and slander

Queen's Counsel

Barristers of at least ten years standing may apply to become queen's counsel. QCs undertake work of an important nature and are referred to as 'silks' which is derived from the Courts gown that is worn. Will be known as king's counsel if a king assumes the throne

R

Re-allocation

Transferring the case from one allocated track to another. This can happen if the value of the case increases

Receiver

Person appointed by the Court of Protection to act on behalf of a patient

Recognisance

An undertaking before the Court by which a person agrees to comply with a certain condition, e.g. keep the peace/appear in court. A sum of money is normally pledged to ensure compliance

Recorder

(also Assistant Recorder) Members of the legal profession (barristers or solicitors) who are appointed to act in a judicial capacity on a part time bases. They may progress to become a full time judge

Redetermintaion (civil)

If the defendant or claimant objects to the rate of repayment set by a court officer, the judge will decide on the matter.

Redetermination (criminal)

An application by a solicitor or counsel for amounts assessed by determination to be reconsidered

Register of judgments, orders and fines

A public register containing details of county court and High Court judgments, fines enforced by magistrates' courts and county court administration orders

Registrar

Registrars and deputy registrars were renamed DISTRICT Judges and Deputy DISTRICT Judges respectively in the Courts and Legal Services Act 1990 Registry Trust Limited

(RTL)

The company contracted to the Ministry of Justice to maintain the Register of Judgments Orders and Fines. You can find out if an individual or a company at a particular address has unsatisfied (unpaid) court judgments against them by searching the Register of Judgments, Orders and Fines. There is a small fee for this. You can get further information about searching the Register from: Registry Trust Ltd, 73-75 Cleveland Street, London, WT 6QR

Released

A witness is released (freed from an obligation or duty) by the court, when he or she has given evidence in a case

Remand

To order an accused person to be kept in custody or placed on bail pending further Court appearance

Respondent (Civil & Crime)

The defending party (person) in an appeal or in a petition to the courts. See also Appellant

Response pack

A response pack is sent to the defendant in a civil claim with the claim form or with the particulars of claim (if they were served separately). The pack contains all the forms needed to reply to the claim

Restitution

Where a defendant who has been evicted by a bailiff illegally re-enters the property the claimant must issue a warrant of restitution with the court in order to regain possession

Right of Audience

Entitlement to appear before a Court in a legal capacity and conduct proceedings on behalf of a party to the proceedings

S

Sanction

A penalty imposed on a person involved in a case if he or she, for example, fails to comply with directions or refuses to consider an alternative to court. Even though a person wins a case, the judge may order them to pay the other party's costs

Satisfaction

Paying a debt or settling an obligation by an act or deed

Security of tenure

A period in which something is held

Service

Delivery by post, or in person, of the claim form, or other court documents

Set aside judgment

See judgment set aside

Settlement

A voluntarily agreement by the claimant and defendant to settle their civil case.

Sheriff

An officer of the Crown whose duties, amongst other things, consist of the enforcement of High Court writs of execution

Skeleton argument

A written summary of the main points of a case to be heard by an appeal court.

SILK

Queens Counsel, a senior barrister sometimes referred to as a leader or leading counsel

SLANDER

Spoken words which have a damaging effect on a person's reputation

Small Claims Track

The path that defended claims of no more than £5,000 (and personal injury and housing disrepair claims of no more than £1,000) are allocated to

Solicitor

Member of the legal profession chiefly concerned with advising clients and preparing their cases and representing them in some Courts. May also act as advocates before certain Courts or tribunals

Specified amounts of money

A specific and easily calculable amount of money, such as a debt owed to a claimant

Specified Claim

A type of claim which is issued for a fixed amount of money allegedly owing. Previously known as a liquidated claim

Statement

A written account by a witness of the facts of details of a matter

Statement of case

The statement of case contains the outline of the claimant's case and includes: (i) a claim form, (ii) the particulars of claim – where these are not included in the claim form; (iii) the defence and (iv) a reply to the defence (v) any counterclaim

Statement of truth

Every statement of case must be verified by a statement of truth, signed by the parties involved. A statement of truth is a statement that says that a party believes the facts they have written down are true

Statutory Instrument

A document issued by the delegated authority (usually a Government Minister or committee) named within an act of parliament which affects the workings of the original Act, e.g. The County Courts Act 1984 confers authority on to the County Court

Rule Committee to make rules relating to the operation of the County Courts act

Stay

A suspension of court proceedings. This remains in effect until an order has been followed. No action may be taken in the case other than an application to have the stay lifted. A case can also be stayed when an offer of payment is accepted or if the court feels it is necessary

Stay of Execution

An order following which judgment cannot be enforced without leave of the court

Striking a case out (striking out)

The court can strike out a case (prevent all further proceedings) if a party fails to comply with a rule, practice direction or court order. It can also happen if it appears there are no reasonable grounds for bringing or defending a claim. Either party (the defendant or the claimant) can ask the court to strike a case out

Subpoena

A summons issued to a person directing their attendance in Court to give evidence

Suit

Legal proceedings commenced by petition

Suitor

Person bringing a suit before the Courts

Summary Assessment (of costs)

When a court makes a cost order it may make a summary assessment of costs immediately after it has made the order. The court will usually make a summary assessment

Summary Judgment

A judgment obtained by a claimant where there is no defence to the case or the defence contains no valid grounds. A summary judgment can be obtained without a trial or hearing. A defendant can also obtain summary judgment if he or she can establish that the claimant has no real prospect of succeeding on the claim. You have to apply to the court for a summary judgement hearing to take place

Summary Offence

A criminal offence which is triable only by a Magistrates Court

Summary procedure

A procedure by which the court when making an order about costs, orders payment of a sum of money instead of fixed costs or detailed assessment

Summing-up

A review of the evidence and directions as to the law by a judge immediately before a jury retires to consider its verdict

Summons

Order to appear or to produce evidence to a court

Summons (Jury)

Order to attend for jury service

Summons (Witness)

Order to appear as a witness at a hearing

Supreme Court of

Judicature

Collective name encompassing - High Court of Justice, Crown Court and Court of Appeal

Surety

A person's undertaking to be liable for another's default or non-attendance at Court

Suspended Sentence

A custodial sentence which will not take effect unless there is a subsequent offence within a specified period

T

Third party

Person who is not party to a legal case, but may be relevant because he or she owes the defendant money. In that case the defendant can issue a third party notice against such a party

Third party debt order

An order issued by a Claimant, against a third party, to seize money or other assets in their keeping, but belonging to the debtor. Orders can be granted preventing a defendant from withdrawing money from their bank or building society account. The money is paid to the claimant from the account. A third party debt order can also be sent to anyone who owes the defendant money

Tipstaff

An officer of the Supreme Court whose duties involve the enforcement of High Court arrest warrants

Tort

An action in tort is a claim for damages to compensate the claimant for harm suffered. Such claims arise from cases of personal injury, breach of contract and damage to personal reputation. As well as damages, remedies include an injunction to prevent harm occurring again

Trial

A public hearing in which the evidence in a case, and the law which applies, are examined

Trial (civil)

Civil trials are generally held before one or more judges without a jury. The form and length of a civil trial will depend on the track to which the case has been allocated

Trial bundles

These are the documents that are likely to be referred to in a trial or tribunal hearing. Identical bundles are prepared for the judge and the parties to the case

Trial contents

The contents of the trial include any written statements and documents in trial bundles

Trial Window

A period of time within which the case must be listed for trial

Tribunal

A tribunal is a body outside of the court structure. They hear disputes relating to specific areas such as immigration, employment and some tax matters and adjudicate on them. Tribunals are thought to be cheap and fast and allow expert knowledge to be applied

Trust

Property legally entrusted to a person with instructions to use it for another person (or persons benefit)

Trustee

A person who holds or administers property in a trust for another (or others)

U

Undertaking

A promise, which can be enforced by law, made by a party (person) or their legal representative during legal proceedings

Unspecified amount of money

An unspecified amount of money is one which is not precise. For example, if you are claiming damages (compensation) for loss or injury, you might not be able to work out exactly what those damages are

Unspecified Claim

A claim where the amount to be awarded is left to the Court to determine, e.g. damages to be assessed for personal injuries. Previously known as an unliquidated claim

V

Varied order

If a defendant has been ordered to pay an amount in full or by instalments, which they cannot afford, they can ask the court to vary the order to allow payment by instalments or by reduced instalments

Verdict

The finding of guilty or not guilty by a jury

Vexatious litigant

A person who regularly brings court cases which have little chance of succeeding. The Attorney General can apply to the High Court for an order to prevent such as person form starting legal proceedings without permission.

Vice Chancellor

judge and head of the Chancery Division of the High Court of Justice (although the Lord Chancellor is the nominal head)

Voluntary

Something is voluntary when it is entered into without compulsion, as a result of the free choice of the person(s) concerned

W

Walking Possession

A signed agreement by a debtor not to remove goods levied by a bailiff under the authority of a warrant of execution and to allow the bailiff access at any time to inspect the goods, in consideration of which the bailiff leaves the goods in the possession of the debtor

Winding up

The voluntary or compulsory closure of a company and the subsequent realisation of assets and payment to creditors

Witness

A person who gives evidence in Court, called to give evidence because they witnesses an event (see also Expert witness)

Witness summons

A document issued by a court which requires a person to give evidence in court or to produce a report or other documentation for the court

About the author

Harry Jones is a highly experienced and well regarded motoring industry professional. He has produced a wide range of books and training materials on transport related subjects. His transport industry experience has taken him all over Europe and he has experience of all sides of the motoring business, as a driver, company vehicle driver, commercial vehicle driver (both passenger and transport)

His clear and concise approach to all matters relating to driving law, including licensing, road safety and legal issues is well known and widely acknowledged within the industry. Harry believes that the future of motoring in the UK lies in fewer regulations and better trained drivers, as well as more government awareness of the rights of the motorist and more sensible police priorities where motoring often appears to take priority over serious crime..

He is married with two children and lives in the UK, where he continues to work within the motoring industry, producing a developing range of training materials. His hobbies include football, he is an avid Manchester United supporter, as well as writing, hiking, sea-angling and spending time with his family.

CPSIA information can be obtained at www.ICGtesting.com
Printed in the USA
BVOW05s1705190314

348163BV00017B/816/P

9 781906 512422